TRAUMA
To Triumph
Supporting Trauma Victims with PTSD,
Anxiety and Depression

Harrison S. Mungal, PhD, PsyD

Foreword by Hannah Rockman, Psy.D., C. Psych

Trauma To Triumph

Contact author via email:
info@agetoage.ca
www.agetoage.ca
www.harrisonmungal.com
www.harrisonmungalbooks.com
Facebook: Harrison Mungal
Twitter: AgeToAgeInc1
LinkedIn: Harrison Mungal, Ph.D., PsyD
YouTube: Harrison Mungal
Phone: 905-533-1334

ABOUT *the*
AUTHOR

Harrison is passionate about life and the people he supports as a therapist with a clinical psychology background. He holds two doctorate degrees, one in Clinical Psychology and the other in Philosophy in Social Work. He has two master's degrees, a master's degree in Social Work and a master's degree in Counselling. And, a Bachelor's degree in Theology. He specializes in mental health, addictions, marriage and relationships, parenting, and the family.

Harrison is considered one of the leading cognitive therapist workshop presenters. He wears many hats in supporting individuals, couples, families, and corporations. He has been a public speaker to over forty-two nations as a keynote speaker at conferences, seminars, and public events, as well as a speaker on several Radio and Television programs. He has written over twenty-five books. He is appreciated for the depth of his knowledge, great humour and passion for relationships, parenting, mental health, addictions, and other related life struggles.

Harrison utilizes a creative scientific-based approach to deliver compelling presentations that have granted him an excellent reputation.

He has received several awards and recognitions from local police, mayors, community leaders, managers and directors, and families. He provides training and consultations to various community partners, including psychiatrists, medical doctors, social workers, nurses, police officers, firefighters and senior management teams.

Harrison has been involved in cognitive research to support individuals with addictions, psychosis, anxiety, and depression. He spearheaded several research studies on various themes, including music therapy and schizophrenia, vaccinations for children under six years old, substance abuse and addiction in the food service industry, and Thought Developmental Practice (TDP). His research on TDP with outpatient provided diversion methods to support substance abuse and addictions, anxiety, and depression under the supervision of the chief of psychiatry, Dr. David Koczerginski.

Harrison has over twenty-one years of professional experience working with diverse populations, including seventeen years in mental health and more than ten years as a psychotherapist. These diverse populations include youth and adult offenders, communities impacted by Acquired Brain Injuries, refugees, war victims, and those needing crisis-based support in various settings, i.e., liaison with police, hospitals, community agencies, and inpatient mental health settings.

Harrison specializes in evidence-based therapies, including Cognitive Behavioural Therapy (CBT), Cognitive Processing Therapy (CPT), Dialectical Behavioural Therapy (DBT), Thought Developmental Practice (TDP), Acceptance and Commitment Therapy (ACT), Interpersonal therapy (IPT), Motivational Interviewing Techniques, Grounding Techniques, Integrative Eclectic Therapy, Humanistic Experiential Therapy, Interpersonal Therapy, Supportive Therapy, Exposure Therapy, Visual Therapy, Psychodynamic Therapy.

FOREWORD

By Dr. Hannah Rockman PsyD.,
C.Psych.

I take great pleasure and felt honoured to give a foreword for the book "Trauma To Triumph." It's an excellent book that shares trauma-related issues, including PTSD—working with first responders, firefighters, police officers, emergency doctors, EMS, paramedics, nurses and others who experience trauma firsthand. This book clarifies trauma with the signs and symptoms, along with coping strategies.

Harrison has done an excellent job in helping the readers understand the severity of trauma and its impact on an individual, their relationship, their family, friends and loved ones. This book has given great insight into what a trauma victim can expect from their loved ones and their employers. It will take you to another level of understanding of how the brain is affected and the importance of restructuring thoughts and reconditioning the mind.

I have been working with Harrison since 2017 and have had numerous feedback from our trauma-related patients/clients regarding the support and insight he has. Harrison has summarized his vast clinical knowledge about PTSD in a book and his experience working with first responders and military personnel. All our patients/clients who are privileged to see him benefit significantly from his positive and structured way of working. He is down to earth and can share what he knows in a way that is easy to relate to meeting them where they are.

The book outlines easy-to-read information about trauma in clear and non-jargon language, which is helpful for professionals and non-professionals who want to understand PTSD and some of the best, well-researched strategies to treat it. You will discover the best treatment options for people recovering from the effects of *trauma with evidence-based therapies. You will be able to* recognize, understand, and empathize with the impact of *trauma*. The book is inspiring; it provides a clear way forward to issues that sometimes seem insurmountable.

I am privileged to know Harrison, who has been one of our most competent clinicians and a good friend.

Dr. Hannah Rockman PsyD., C.Psych.

Hannah is the Founder and Principal of YRPS. She is a member of the College of Psychologists of Ontario, the British Psychological Society, the Ontario Psychological Association and the National Academy of Neuropsychology.

She has extensive experience in counselling in Canada, England and Israel at hospitals, clinics and private healthcare.

Hannah has over 20 years of experience working with clients involved in personal injury, motor vehicle and work-related accidents. She has conducted assessments for Medical/Rehabilitation, Psycho-vocational assessments, Disability and Catastrophic Impairment in the context of Independent Medical Examinations and working with clients and their legal representatives.

In addition, Hannah works with individuals, couples and children of all ages. She conducts neuropsychological, ADHD, immigration, psycho-educational and gifted assessments for individuals. Hannah has also been involved in infertility counselling for several fertility clinics.

Having practiced on three continents, Dr. Rockman is experienced in dealing with populations from diverse cultural backgrounds.

TABLE *Of* CONTENT

ABOUT THE AUTHOR 3

INTRODUCTION 9

TRAUMA 11

PTSD 15

COMPLEX TRAUMA 21

EMOTIONAL AND PSYCHOLOGICAL TRAUMA? 27

THE MIND, WILL AND EMOTIONS 31

TRAUMA AND THE BODY 35

NIGHTMARES, FLASHBACKS, AND INTRUSIVE THOUGHTS 47

HYPERVIGILANT 51

STUCKPOINTS 55

TRIGGERS 63

SUPPORT SYSTEM 73

RETURN TO WORK 85

CONCLUSION 89

REFERENCES... 91

INTRODUCTION

In its vast complexity, human life presents a kaleidoscope of experiences—some that uplift us and others that cause profound distress. When these distressing experiences reach a certain degree of severity, they can lead to what psychological science refers to as 'trauma.' Trauma is not just an isolated experience; it is a condition that can have wide-ranging and long-lasting effects on an individual's mental health, physical well-being, and social relationships (American Psychological Association, 2013).

"Trauma to Triumph" is a comprehensive guide designed to explore the intricacies of traumatic experiences and illuminate the path to recovery. This book goes beyond theoretical insights; it serves as a practical roadmap for those affected by trauma, drawing from a rich body of empirical research and evidence-based interventions.

The objective of this guide is not to paint an unrealistic picture of a life devoid of distress—such an outlook would be an oversimplification of the human experience. Instead, the purpose is to equip readers with a robust understanding of trauma, its manifestations, and the tools necessary to navigate recovery.

This book delves deep into trauma, dissecting its various types and exploring its impact on the human psyche. We examine acute trauma, which results from single distressing events; chronic trauma, which arises from repeated and prolonged adverse experiences; and complex trauma, which results from exposure to multiple and varied traumatic events (Centre for Addiction and Mental Health, 2019).

The exploration doesn't end with understanding the nature and types of traumas. This book also serves as a beacon of hope for those recovering from traumatic experiences. Drawing from a wealth of scientific literature, we discuss evidence-based coping strategies, underscore the critical importance of professional intervention, and highlight the nurturing power of supportive communities in the healing process.

A crucial aspect of this guide is the comprehensive exploration of Post Traumatic Stress Disorder (PTSD), a psychological condition often associated with traumatic experiences. PTSD, once misunderstood and stigmatized, is now recognized as a severe mental health condition that requires professional intervention. We strive to demystify PTSD by providing in-depth insights into its causes, symptoms, and evidence-backed treatment strategies (National Institute of Mental Health, 2019).

The ultimate aim is for you to gain knowledge and develop a transformative perspective on trauma and resilience. Armed with this knowledge and understanding, readers will be better equipped to transform the adversity of trauma into a triumph of resilience, turning distressing experiences into catalysts for personal growth and self-improvement.

You have chosen to confront the adversity of trauma and seek pathways to recovery. This guide is here to assist you every step of the way, offering empirical insights and practical strategies to facilitate your journey toward healing and self-discovery.

TRAUMA

Understanding trauma requires more than just a cursory glance at its definition. It involves delving into the intricacies of its nature, types, and impacts on individuals. This chapter aims to provide a comprehensive overview of trauma, enabling readers to grasp its complexity and profound influence on human life.

Trauma, as defined by the American Psychological Association (APA), is an emotional response to a terrible event such as an accident, rape, or natural disaster (American Psychological Association, 2013). However, this definition only scratches the surface of what trauma entails. Trauma is a complex psychological state that can have long-lasting effects on an individual's mental, physical, and social well-being. It typically arises from experiences threatening an individual's life, safety, or physical integrity.

Trauma is not a monolithic construct; it manifests in various forms, each with distinct characteristics and implications for the affected individual. Broadly, trauma can be categorized into three main types: acute, chronic, and complex (Centre for Addiction and Mental Health, 2019).

Acute trauma arises from a single, distressing event. This form of trauma is typically associated with sudden and unexpected occurrences that significantly threaten an individual's safety or life. Examples of events that can lead to acute trauma include natural disasters like earthquakes or hurricanes, physical or sexual assault, sudden loss of a loved one, or involvement in a severe accident (American Psychiatric Association, 2013). Traumas from exposing this mind to images involving crimes, motor vehicle accidents, witnessing deaths and other disturbing images that creates memory cards. Some traumas are formulated from hearing others share their traumas, called vicarious traumas.

In the event's immediate aftermath, individuals may experience a range of intense emotional and physical reactions. These can include shock, confusion, disorientation, fear, and physical symptoms like trembling, heart palpitations, or nausea. Acute trauma can also lead to the development of acute stress disorder (ASD), a condition characterized by severe distress and functional impairment occurring within a month of exposure to a traumatic event (Meiser-Stedman et al., 2017).

Chronic trauma, on the other hand, is the result of prolonged and repeated exposure to distressing events. This trauma often arises in domestic violence, prolonged warfare, or long-term child abuse. Chronic trauma can also occur in neglect or ongoing emotional abuse (Stubley & Young, 2021).

The repeated nature of a traumatic event can lead to a cumulative impact on the individual, leading to severe psychological distress and impairment. Chronic trauma can contribute to the development of complex PTSD, a condition characterized by symptoms of PTSD, along with additional symptoms like emotional dysregulation, negative self-perception, and interpersonal problems (Jowett et al., 2020).

Complex trauma refers to exposure to multiple traumatic events, often of an invasive and interpersonal nature. This type of trauma usually involves a degree of captivity, where the individual does not have the freedom to escape the distressing circumstances. Complex trauma is often experienced by individuals subjected to prolonged abuse or neglect, particularly during childhood (Maercker, 2022).

Complex trauma can pervasively affect an individual's identity, relationships, and physical health. Individuals with complex trauma often struggle with issues such as difficulties regulating emotions, disturbances in consciousness and memory, distorted perceptions of perpetrators, and difficulties sustaining relationships.

The impact of trauma is not limited to specific individuals but extends to various professions and life situations. For example, emergency responders, including Police officers, firefighters, EMS, and other workers, regularly face traumatic situations that can affect their mental well-being. Healthcare Professionals like Nurses and doctors experience trauma through continuous exposure to suffering, emergencies, and death. Even people involved in severe accidents (motor vehicle accidents, industrial accidents, etc.) suffer from trauma that can have lasting effects. The immense grief and trauma experienced from personal events, including those who have lost a baby, can have profound and enduring impacts.

The negative impact of trauma extends beyond the immediate emotional response to the distressing event. Trauma can lead to various short-term and long-term effects on an individual's physical health, mental health, and overall quality of life (National Institute of Mental Health, 2019). Trauma's impact is also shaped by visual and auditory information. Disturbing images and sounds can create lasting memories, leading to long-term distress and altering how we think and perceive the world.

Short-term effects may include shock, denial, confusion, and difficulty concentrating. Over time, if the trauma is not appropriately addressed, individuals may experience more severe and persistent symptoms such as depression, anxiety, post-traumatic stress disorder

(PTSD), and even physical health problems like chronic pain and sleep disturbances.

Understanding trauma's nature, types, and impacts is essential for creating effective coping and recovery strategies. This comprehensive exploration lays the groundwork for further discussions on trauma intervention, healing, resilience, and community support, focusing on real-world applications and support mechanisms.

We have explored the definition of trauma, its various types, and its potential impacts. This foundational knowledge will serve as the base for our subsequent discussions on coping strategies, professional intervention, and community support.

PTSD

Post Traumatic Stress Disorder (PTSD) is a mental health condition that can develop after exposure to a traumatic event. PTSD is often associated with life-threatening events such as warfare, violent personal assaults, or natural disasters. However, it's important to note that not everyone who experiences a traumatic event will develop PTSD. The manifestation of PTSD is a complex interplay of individual vulnerability, coping mechanisms, and the nature of the traumatic event (American Psychiatric Association, 2013).

Individuals with PTSD may have changes in physical and emotional reactions as they become easily startled or frightened—an unexpected loud noise could cause them to jump or scream. They may have difficulty sleeping, frequently waking up throughout the night or having trouble falling asleep due to anxiety or nightmares. Aggressive or self-destructive behaviour can also manifest—a normally calm person might start getting into fights, or someone might start drinking excessively as a coping mechanism, using illicit drugs to cope. Hypervigilance is very common, with the feeling of being highly or abnormally alert. They may feel they are in potential danger or threat, heightened with startle responses.

Victims who have PTSD may experience re-experiencing symptoms, which involve the individual reliving the traumatic event in various forms. These symptoms can be incredibly distressing, causing the person to feel as though the event is happening all over again (Hall et al., 2018). It includes recurring memories that are persistent, disturbing memories of an incident. Intrusive thoughts invade the mind during everyday activities.

Nightmares are prevalent from incidents that were visual and auditory. A car accident survivor may experience nightmares about the crash, disrupting their sleep and causing anxiety.

Flashbacks are very common, creating anxiety and fear. A victim of assault might suddenly feel they're back in the moment of their attack during a triggered episode. This can happen anytime and can be prompted by sights, sounds, or smells that remind them of the event.

Avoidance symptoms in PTSD lead individuals to actively evade reminders of the traumatic event, causing them to change their behaviour and lifestyle to minimize exposure to triggering situations.

Avoiding transportation when involved in an MVA is very common. Someone in a severe car accident may avoid driving or even riding in cars, leading to significant challenges in daily life. They would need therapy to reintegrate into driving or being in a vehicle to avoid anxiety. The same idea applies to someone who experienced trauma in a crowded place. They may prevent busy areas like shopping malls or public events, limiting social interactions and possibly affecting their mental well-being.

PTSD can cause a range of adverse alterations in thoughts and mood, including developing negative beliefs, loss of interest in hobbies, and irrational feelings of guilt or blame. There are adverse changes in thinking, behaviours and mood. Some individuals with PTSD may have a fixed belief that they're a terrible person or that the world is entirely dangerous, leading to anxiety and depression.

Some individuals may feel guilt and shame, carrying negative beliefs. Survivors may irrationally blame themselves for being unable to prevent it, even though it was beyond their control. They explore in their minds all the different things they could have done to avoid an accident or any incident that created PTSD.

There may be a loss of interest, where isolation and a decreased quality of life become the new normal. Individuals with PTSD may not want to socialize or be around people, as they may not want to share their trauma stories or be triggered by questions.

There may be changes in physical and emotional reactions as PTSD can lead to alterations in physical and emotional responses, making trauma individuals more susceptible to startling stimuli, sleep disturbances, and even aggressive or self-destructive behaviour.

Some people living with PTSD can be easily startled by unexpected loud noise. They can become "jumpy, hypervigilant, angry and frustrated, making daily life more stressful. Their neurovegetative state of mind can be altered, affecting their eating habits sleeping patterns with difficulty waking throughout the night or trouble falling asleep due to anxiety or nightmares.

A normally calm person might start getting into fights. Substance and illicit drug use can become very common, developing addictions.

PTSD often does not occur in isolation. It is frequently accompanied by other psychiatric disorders, a phenomenon known as comorbidity. Understanding these comorbid conditions is crucial as they can complicate the diagnosis and treatment of PTSD and often contribute to the severity of an individual's distress and impairment (Raise-Abdullahi et al., 2023).

Major depressive disorder is one of the most common conditions co-occurring with PTSD. The shared symptoms of PTSD and depression, such as difficulty sleeping and concentration problems, can complicate the diagnostic process. Moreover, depression can exacerbate the distress experienced by individuals with PTSD and increase the risk of suicide.

PTSD can co-occur with various anxiety disorders, including generalized anxiety disorder (GAD), panic disorder, and social anxiety disorder. These anxiety disorders can worsen the anxiety symptoms associated with PTSD, making it more difficult for individuals to manage their symptoms.

Many individuals with PTSD struggle with substance use disorders. This is often an attempt to self-medicate, as substances may temporarily alleviate some of the distressing symptoms of PTSD. However, substance use can exacerbate PTSD symptoms in the long run and lead to additional problems, including physical health issues and interpersonal problems.

Individuals with PTSD are also at an increased risk of experiencing somatic symptoms, such as chronic pain and gastrointestinal problems. They are also more likely to have medical conditions like heart disease, diabetes, and respiratory disorders. The reasons for this are complex and likely involve a combination of factors, including the physiological stress response, health behaviours, and access to healthcare.

Despite the severe impact of PTSD on an individual's life, there is hope in the form of effective treatments. These primarily include psychotherapy, medication, or a combination of both (National Institute of Mental Health, 2019).

Healing from PTSD is a complex and gradual process that often requires professional intervention and ongoing support. The journey toward recovery can be slow, and it's vital to recognize that patience, persistence, and individualized care are often needed.

Several practical therapeutic approaches for treating PTSD address specific symptoms and underlying issues, including Cognitive-Behavioral Therapy (CBT). One of the most effective forms of psychotherapy for PTSD, CBT, focuses on changing thought patterns that lead to harmful behaviours or emotions. Individuals can develop healthier coping strategies and reduce symptoms by identifying and challenging negative thoughts and beliefs.

Eye Movement Desensitization and Reprocessing (EMDR): EMDR involves processing traumatic memories in a new way to reduce their distressing impact. By guiding the patient's eye movements while recounting the traumatic event, therapists can help the individual reframe and integrate the memory, lessening its emotional toll (Bisson et al., 2013). Understanding the available treatments and how they work is essential for those affected by PTSD and the healthcare professionals working with them.

PTSD is a severe and multifaceted mental health condition, but healing is possible with the proper support and therapeutic interventions. It's essential to approach treatment with compassion and an understanding of the time it may take for an individual to recover truly. Recovery is often not a linear path, and setbacks may occur, but continued support and appropriate therapy can lead to profound healing and a return to a fulfilling life.

COMPLEX TRAUMA

Complex trauma is a form of trauma that occurs repeatedly and cumulatively, usually over a period of time and within specific relationships and contexts. Unlike single-incident traumas (which are limited to one event), complex traumas are typically invasive, interpersonal in nature, and often occur at developmentally vulnerable times in the victim's life, such as early childhood or adolescence (Cook et al., 2005).

Complex trauma is often associated with circumstances where the victim has an existing relationship with the perpetrator, such as in child abuse, domestic violence, or long-term exploitation. It can also occur in situations where the individual cannot escape, leading to a prolonged period of traumatic experience (Courtois, 2004).

Complex trauma's repetitive and prolonged nature can lead to more severe symptoms than single-incident trauma. It can profoundly affect a person's sense of self and relationships with others. The effects are often wide-ranging and long-term, affecting many aspects of the individual's life and identity (Cloitre et al., 2009).

Complex trauma results from multiple and sustained traumatic events, often of an invasive, interpersonal nature. This can create a pattern of psychological harm that extends beyond the symptoms of traditional PTSD. The effects of complex trauma are pervasive, affecting the individual's identity, relationships, and overall well-being. It often requires specialized treatment to address the deep-rooted issues and facilitate healing.

Complex trauma usually stems from child abuse and neglect; physical abuse, including constant physical violence or threat of violence; sexual abuse, including repeated sexual exploitation or assault; emotional abuse, chronic verbal abuse, humiliation, or emotional neglect and neglect in general from basic needs, including food, safety, education, and emotional connection.

We can be traumatized by domestic violence and witnessing violence, especially for children who witness violence between parents, caregivers, friends and extended families. Some of us may have been traumatized from trafficking and exploitation or other forms of servitude, community violence and war, orphanages and foster care, and many negative impacts on the emotional being.

Complex trauma can result in various symptoms and effects, similar to PTSD, but also include additional features. These symptoms often reflect the chronic and pervasive nature of the traumatic experiences (Cloitre et al., 2009; Ford & Courtois, 2009).

Individuals who have experienced complex trauma may struggle to manage their emotions effectively. They may feel emotions more intensely, have more rapid and intense emotional reactions, and take longer to return to a calm state. For instance, they might experience severe depression, pervasive sadness, hopelessness, and a lack of interest in things they once enjoyed. Anxiety disorders, characterized by excessive and persistent worry, are also common. They might struggle with intense anger, feeling irritable and short-tempered, and having difficulty controlling their anger.

Complex trauma can lead to disruptions in consciousness and attention, often manifesting as dissociative symptoms. For example, an individual might feel disconnected from their thoughts, memories, or identity or detached from their physical presence (depersonalization). They could also experience derealization, where the world seems unreal or dreamlike. In addition, complex trauma often impacts memory, leading to difficulties in recalling key features of traumatic events or leading to intrusive and unwanted memories of the trauma.

Complex trauma often leads to a negative self-concept. Victims might see themselves as helpless or damaged beyond repair. For instance, a survivor of childhood abuse might carry guilt and shame into adulthood, believing they were somehow responsible for the misuse or that the abuse has left them permanently flawed.

Victims of complex trauma may develop distorted views of their perpetrator. They might attribute total power to the perpetrator, believing they have complete control over them even long after the traumatic situation ends. Alternatively, they might become preoccupied with thoughts of revenge, which can fuel anger and bitterness and impede the healing process.

Complex trauma often creates significant challenges in forming and maintaining healthy relationships. A person repeatedly betrayed by trusted figures might find it hard to trust others, fearing further victimization. They might struggle with intimacy, keeping others at a distance to protect themselves from potential harm. These difficulties can lead to a cycle of isolation and further psychological distress.

Victims of complex trauma may experience physical symptoms that can't be explained by a medical condition, a phenomenon known as somatization. These real symptoms can cause significant distress, even though they originate from psychological distress rather than a physical disease. Examples include chronic pain, digestive issues, headaches, or unexplained neurological problems like numbness or tremors.

Treatment for complex trauma typically necessitates an approach that addresses the broad spectrum of the trauma's effects, considering the pervasive impact on the individual's life. Given the complexity and severity of symptoms associated with complex trauma, a combination of therapeutic modalities is often employed.

Trauma-Focused Cognitive Behavioural Therapy (TF-CBT). This form of therapy helps individuals understand and change thought patterns leading to destructive behaviours and emotions. The therapist assists the client in identifying thoughts and beliefs that are harmful or inaccurate, then helps them challenge and replace these with healthier, more realistic ones. For example, a therapist might help a client replace the belief "I deserved the abuse" with "No one deserves to be mistreated."

Dialectical Behaviour Therapy (DBT). Originally developed to treat Borderline Personality Disorder, DBT is often used in complex trauma because it focuses on emotional regulation, mindfulness, and interpersonal effectiveness. DBT teaches skills to manage painful emotions and decrease conflict in relationships. For instance, clients might learn techniques to help them stay calm and effectively express their needs during a disagreement rather than resorting to destructive behaviours.

Eye Movement Desensitization and Reprocessing (EMDR). This is a unique, evidence-based therapy for PTSD, including complex trauma. It involves the client recalling traumatic memories while the therapist guides them in making specific eye movements. This process is thought to facilitate reprocessing traumatic memories, reducing their emotional intensity. For example, a person who has been avoiding reminders of their trauma might find that, after EMDR, they can think about the traumatic event without experiencing intense distress. Somatic therapies. These are body-centred therapies that aim to treat the physiological aspects of trauma. Somatic therapies can include somatic experiencing, which focuses on bodily sensations to help resolve trauma, or sensorimotor psychotherapy, which integrates talk therapy with physical interventions. For example, a client might learn to notice when their body shows signs of stress or fear (like muscle tension or rapid breathing) and then use grounding techniques to calm their body down.

We can focus on several areas of treatment, including enhancing safety which is the priority to ensure the client is safe and not currently in a traumatic situation. This might involve practical assistance (like help finding safe housing) and psychological work (like developing a safety plan for potential suicidal thoughts).

Victims of traumas often learn skills to help manage intense emotions, including mindfulness, distress tolerance, and self-soothing techniques.

Processing traumatic memories is another technique used once the trauma victim is in a safer and more stable place emotionally; treatment often involves gradually facing and processing traumatic memories rather than avoiding them.

Therapy often focuses on building healthier relationships, which might involve learning about boundaries, effective communication, and trust. (Courtois & Ford, 2009).

It's essential to recognize that complex trauma is not our fault. The causes are often systemic and rooted in circumstances beyond our control. Understanding the origins of complex trauma helps devise targeted interventions and support systems to aid recovery.

EMOTIONAL *and* PSYCHOLOGICAL TRAUMA?

Emotional and psychological trauma form a significant part of our understanding of the overall concept of trauma. While these terms are often used interchangeably, they entail different aspects of the human response to distressing events. This chapter aims to dissect these types of trauma, investigating their definitions, causes, effects, and intricate interplay.

Emotional trauma is a response to a highly distressing event or series of events that exceeds an individual's ability to cope or integrate the resulting emotions into their current reality (Briere & Scott, 2014). This type of trauma may stem from a wide range of experiences, such as a car accident, a natural disaster, the sudden death of a loved one, or a violent assault.

When people undergo emotional trauma, their usual coping mechanisms may fail, causing intense fear, sadness, despair, and hopelessness. Emotional trauma can sometimes lead to physical symptoms like headaches, nausea, and fatigue. It can also disrupt cognitive functions, causing difficulty concentrating, memory problems, and confusion.

Over time, if not addressed, emotional trauma can result in more serious mental health problems, such as depression, anxiety, and post-traumatic stress disorder (PTSD). Therefore, understanding and addressing emotional trauma is critical to healing and recovery (van der Kolk, 2014).

Psychological trauma, however, is a type of damage that occurs to the psyche following a severely distressing event. This form of trauma can lead to the development of mental health disorders, including PTSD, acute stress disorder, adjustment disorders, and various conditions of anxiety and depressive disorders (American Psychiatric Association, 2013).

The causes of psychological trauma are diverse and can range from a single, isolated event, such as a violent assault, to long-term, chronic exposure to abuse or neglect. The severity and duration of psychological trauma can depend on multiple factors, including the nature of the traumatic event, the individual's personal history and psychological makeup, and the availability of social support.

The effects of psychological trauma can be profound and long-lasting, impacting various aspects of an individual's life. These effects may include difficulties in emotional regulation, distorted perceptions of the self and others, feelings of helplessness and hopelessness, and a pervasive sense of threat or danger. In some cases, psychological trauma can also lead to dissociation, a psychological response characterized by a disconnection from one's thoughts, feelings, memories, or sense of identity (Briere & Scott, 2014).

Emotional and psychological trauma are closely intertwined, often co-occurring and influencing each other. For instance, an emotionally traumatic event can lead to psychological trauma and vice versa. Moreover, the emotional responses during a traumatic event can shape the psychological impact of that event and the individual's subsequent mental health (van der Kolk, 2014).

However, it is essential to note that the relationship between emotional and psychological trauma is not always linear. Various factors can influence how a traumatic event is processed emotionally and psychologically, including the individual's resilience, support network, and coping strategies.

Moreover, emotional trauma can imprint on an individual's psychological state, affecting their thoughts, behaviours, and overall well-being. Conversely, psychological trauma can impact the emotional state, influencing an individual's capacity to experience, express, and manage emotions.

Understanding the nuances of emotional and psychological trauma is a critical step towards comprehensive trauma-informed care. While distinct in their definitions, these forms of trauma share a complex interplay that can profoundly influence an individual's life. By deepening our understanding of these aspects of trauma, we can better equip ourselves to support those on their healing journey, providing empathetic and effective care.

In the next chapter, we will delve into the impacts of trauma on the mind, will, and emotions, further exploring the wide-reaching effects of traumatic experiences.

THE MIND, *will* AND EMOTIONS

In understanding trauma, exploring its impact on our minds, will, and emotions is essential. These three facets of human experience form the core of our mental and emotional life, influencing how we think, feel, act, and interact with the world around us. This chapter aims to dissect the effects of trauma on these crucial aspects, providing insights into the profound ways trauma can reshape an individual's mental and emotional landscape.

Trauma can significantly impact cognitive functions, including memory, concentration, and decision-making processes (Danese & McEwen, 2012). Exposure to traumatic events can lead to alterations in memory processing, such as intrusive recollections or flashbacks. These can result in the individual repeatedly reliving the traumatic event, contributing to ongoing distress and impairment (Brewin, Gregory, Lipton, & Burgess, 2010).

Further, trauma can interfere with concentration and attention. Our exposure to trauma may lead to difficulty focusing, making us easily distracted. This can affect our ability to perform tasks, engage in problem-solving, or absorb new information.

Moreover, trauma can impact our decision-making processes. Some of us may exhibit impulsive behaviour or struggle with making decisions, often due to heightened fear and perceived threats (Patel, Spreng, Shin, & Girard, 2012).

Trauma can also profoundly affect our will, often associated with our autonomy, motivation, and sense of control. Experiences of trauma often involve situations where our independence is compromised or violated, which can lead to feelings of helplessness and loss of control.

This perceived loss of control can undermine our sense of self-efficacy, affecting our motivation to engage in activities we previously enjoyed or found meaningful. Over time, this can contribute to developing depressive symptoms, such as anhedonia and withdrawal from social activities (Nolen-Hoeksema & Watkins, 2011).

Trauma has a significant impact on our emotional regulation and emotional experiences. Following a traumatic event, we can experience intense negative emotional states like fear, sadness, anger, guilt, or shame (van der Kolk, 2014).

Moreover, trauma can lead to emotional dysregulation, manifesting difficulty in identifying, expressing, and managing emotions. Some may become hypersensitive to emotional stimuli, resulting in intense and often overwhelming emotional reactions. Others may engage in emotional avoidance, numbing their feelings or detaching from their emotional experiences to cope with distress (Cloitre, Miranda, Stovall-McClough, & Han, 2005).

Our minds, willpower, and emotions are not independent entities operating in isolation; they are intricately intertwined, interacting and influencing each other in complex ways, especially in the context of trauma. Understanding this interplay is crucial for a comprehensive grasp of the profound impact of trauma on an individual's life.

Cognitive changes resulting from trauma can significantly affect emotional experiences. For instance, intrusive memories or flashbacks can trigger intense emotional reactions, leading to fear, anger, or sadness (Brewin et al., 2010). This emotional response can, in turn, reinforce the intrusive memory, creating a vicious cycle that perpetuates distress and impairs recovery. Similarly, difficulties with concentration and decision-making can increase feelings of frustration or fear, further contributing to emotional dysregulation.

On the other hand, emotional dysregulation can impact cognitive processes. For instance, intense emotional reactions can overload cognitive resources, making it harder to concentrate or make decisions (Cloitre et al., 2005). Additionally, emotional avoidance or numbing, often used as a coping strategy to manage overwhelming emotions, can lead to a disconnection from one's experiences, impairing the ability to process information and learn from experiences.

The "will," often manifested as our sense of control and autonomy, can also be influenced by cognitive and emotional changes following trauma. For example, intrusive memories and emotional dysregulation can undermine our sense of control, leading to feelings of helplessness or hopelessness. This perceived loss of control can further exacerbate cognitive impairment and emotional dysregulation, creating a self-perpetuating cycle that can compound the effects of trauma.

Moreover, the "will" can also influence cognitive and emotional processes. Our motivation and sense of control can shape how we process traumatic experiences and manage our emotional responses. For instance, feeling in control can promote adaptive coping strategies, such as problem-solving and emotional regulation, facilitating recovery and resilience (Foa, Huppert, & Cahill, 2006).

Our minds, "wills," and emotions are deeply interconnected, forming a complex system where each component influences and is influenced by the others. The mind, encompassing cognitive processes and thought patterns, can shape how trauma is perceived and remembered. The "will," reflecting our determination and choices, can affect our ability to cope with trauma and seek help. Our emotions, ranging from fear and anger to guilt and sadness, play a crucial role in how trauma is experienced and processed. This intricate relationship between our minds, "wills," and emotions creates a unique response to traumatic events, which highly individualizes the experience and recovery process.

Understanding the intricate interplay between our minds, "wills," and emotions in trauma is critical for developing effective interventions and supports when impacted by trauma. Therapy and treatment are considered the unique ways these components interact within each person, tailoring interventions to address the specific needs, beliefs, and emotional responses. By recognizing and working with the interconnectedness of these aspects, mental health professionals can create more personalized and holistic treatment plans. This approach fosters a more comprehensive healing process, allowing trauma victims to rebuild their lives and move forward with resilience and hope.

TRAUMA *and* THE BODY

In our exploration of trauma, we have thus far focused on its psychological and emotional aspects. However, trauma is not solely a mental or emotional phenomenon; it can also profoundly impact our physical health. This chapter delves into the physiological impacts of trauma, shedding light on the intricate connection between mental and physical health and outlining the potential long-term physical consequences of trauma.

When an individual experiences a traumatic event, the body immediately reacts to protect itself. This response often called the fight-or-flight response, is a survival mechanism designed to help us respond to perceived threats. In response to trauma, the body produces stress hormones, including adrenaline and cortisol, which prepare the body for rapid action. Heart rate and blood pressure increase, breathing becomes faster, and muscles tense up, preparing the body to confront or escape the danger (American Psychological Association, 2013).

At the same time, the brain also reacts to trauma. Specifically, the amygdala, an area of the brain involved in emotion processing, sends a distress signal to the hypothalamus, which acts like a command center, communicating with the rest of the body through the nervous system. This communication triggers the fight-or-flight response (National Institute of Mental Health, 2020).

The mind-body connection is a fundamental aspect of human health. This connection implies that our mental and physical health are not separate entities but are deeply intertwined. Mental health issues arising from trauma can lead to various physical health problems. For instance, individuals with post-traumatic stress disorder (PTSD) often experience physical symptoms such as chronic pain, fatigue, and sleep disturbances (Sareen, 2007).

Moreover, the physiological responses to trauma can contribute to mental health issues. For example, the prolonged activation of the stress response system can lead to wear and tear on the body, a process known as allostatic load. Over time, high allostatic load can contribute to various health problems, including heart disease, diabetes, and immune system disorders. These physical health issues can, in turn, exacerbate mental health problems, creating a vicious cycle of worsening psychological and physical health (Danese & McEwen, 2012).

The physiological impacts of trauma can persist long after the traumatic event has passed. Chronic stress associated with trauma can lead to long-lasting changes in the body. For instance, trauma can alter the brain's structure and function, particularly in areas related to memory, emotion regulation, and threat perception (Teicher, Samson, Anderson, & Ohashi, 2016).

Moreover, research has found that trauma can increase the risk of various physical health problems, including cardiovascular disease, diabetes, gastrointestinal disorders, and chronic pain. Additionally, trauma can disrupt sleep patterns, contribute to unhealthy lifestyle behaviours, including substance use and overeating, and lead to poor adherence to medical regimens, further exacerbating physical health problems (Sledjeski, Speisman, & Dierker, 2008).

For example, First responders like firefighters, police officers, EMS, and military soldiers are often exposed to traumatic events as part of their professional duties. The mental trauma they experience can translate into physical symptoms, including chronic fatigue, muscle tension, headaches, and gastrointestinal issues.

A firefighter who has witnessed a tragic loss in a fire or a police officer who witnessed the death of young children might have insomnia and persistent muscle aches, reflecting the body's response to the ongoing mental distress. Military personnel returning from combat zones might experience physical tremors or palpitations, manifestations of underlying anxiety or PTSD.

Similarly, nurses and doctors working in high-stress environments, including emergency rooms, may face physical manifestations of trauma, including sleep disturbances, weight changes, or even chronic pain conditions.

School teachers dealing with traumatic events within the school community might struggle with migraines or digestive problems, reflecting the toll that stress takes on their physical health.

Individuals involved in motor vehicle accidents, even if not physically injured, may develop physical symptoms like dizziness, difficulty breathing, or nausea as part of the body's response to the traumatic event.

The loss of a baby is an intensely painful and traumatic experience that can have significant physical repercussions. The profound grief and mental anguish associated with such a loss may lead to physical symptoms like loss of appetite, sleep disorders, weakened immune function, and even cardiovascular problems.

The mind-body connection in this context illustrates how deeply intertwined mental trauma and physical health can be, requiring compassionate and holistic care to address both the emotional pain and the physical ailments.

Understanding the physiological impacts of trauma highlights the intricate interplay between our mental and physical health. Trauma is not just a psychological phenomenon; it affects our body, alters our brain, and can lead to various physical health problems. As we continue our journey to understand and navigate the aftermath of trauma, it is crucial to remember this interconnectedness. A comprehensive approach to healing from trauma should address the psychological and emotional wounds and the physical ones.

In the next chapter, we will delve into the complex phenomena of nightmares, flashbacks, and intrusive thoughts, further exploring the profound and wide-reaching impacts of traumatic experiences.

THE NEUROSCIENCE
Behind EMOTIONAL WOUNDS

Ever wonder how the brain responds to negative and positive influences? Let's delve deeper into the science behind our minds that have been emotionally wounded from traumas and abuses. Let's explore the role of cognitive dissonance and confirmation bias in maintaining the brain being affected and impacted by our environment. Cognitive dissonance occurs when an individual's beliefs, attitudes, and behaviours are inconsistent or conflicting. In the case of abuse, emotional wounds affect a person's existing core beliefs, and initial values are replaced with new ones that align with the new ideology or agenda. Confirmation bias is a psychological mechanism that contributes to a negative mind. It is the tendency to seek out information confirming one's beliefs while ignoring or dismissing information contradicting them.

Abused individuals often seek information supporting their beliefs and ignore or reject information that challenges them. Those with a wounded emotional mind may believe that a specific group of people (culture, ethnicity, sex, age group, demographics) are evil because of a passed-down mentality or perhaps one bad experience with one wrong person, resulting in cognitive dissonance. They may have triggers when they meet someone kind and friendly from that group. To resolve this dissonance, the brain may rationalize the person's behaviour as an exception or interpret their actions negatively to maintain the belief system. This, however, does lead to discomfort and psychological stress. By understanding the mechanisms behind wounded emotions, we can better equip ourselves to resist future traumas, vicarious traumas, and abuses that affect our mental health. We need to protect ourselves and our emotional minds.

Understanding the anatomy and functioning of the brain concerning thought processes and a negative mind is crucial. The brain is a complex and intricate organ that controls our thoughts, actions, and emotions. It is made up of several parts, each with its unique function. The brain operates through a complex network of neurons, or nerve cells, which communicate with each other through chemical and electrical signals. Neurons form networks and pathways that control specific functions, allowing the brain to process information and produce responses.

In the 1960s, the Triune Brain model was introduced by neuroscientist Paul D. MacLean. It was suggested that the brain can be divided into three main parts: the Reptilian brain, which houses our survival instincts and manages autonomic body processes like breathing, heart rate, thirst, and hunger (Lebow, H. I. 2021). The mammalian brain contains the limbic system, which regulates attachment and reproduction and processes our emotions like joy and fear. (The limbic system is another critical part of the brain that plays a crucial role in our emotions and memory. It comprises several structures, including the amygdala, hippocampus, and hypothalamus. The amygdala processes emotions like fear, anger, and pleasure, while the hippocampus plays a vital role in memory formation and retrieval.

The hypothalamus controls our body's functions, like hunger, thirst, and temperature.) The third part of the brain is the Neomammalian brain, which is responsible for learning, sensory processing, decision-making, memory, and complex problem-solving (Lebow, H. I. 2021).

How our brain processes and interprets information influences our thought processes and thinking. Positive or negative experiences can affect the brain's neural pathways, strengthening or weakening them over time. A positive experience can create new neural pathways, while a negative experience can reinforce existing pathways, leading to a particular thought pattern or mindset. Understanding how the brain processes and stores information is essential to developing strategies for reprogramming the brain and cultivating a positive attitude. We can reshape our neural pathways with the proper techniques and tools, allowing us to adopt a more positive and empowering mindset.

A mind that has been impacted by negative experiences in life, like traumas, abuses, and negative criticism, results in psychological and physiological manifestations. This is a sign from our body that our emotions have been wounded. Psychological mechanisms, including cognitive dissonance, confirmation bias, and social influence, play a crucial role in developing and maintaining a negative mind. The physiological mechanisms release stress hormones, and the amygdala activation reinforces a negative mind.

Social influence is a powerful psychological mechanism that can contribute to a wounded emotion. Group pressure, social isolation, the spoken word, and manipulation of others can influence the beliefs and behaviours of someone emotionally wounded. Someone who is emotionally wounded can be like a tomato. They are sweet and juicy on the inside but have thin skin. They can feel the negative connotations in everything spoken, and anything connected to their sensory nerve (sight, hearing, touching, smelling, and tasting) can exacerbate the hurt they are experiencing.

It is essential to address any challenges or issues we encounter in the present to avoid reinforcing our usual way of thinking and to change the way we will handle our thought processes in the future. This will increase the window of tolerance as the nervous system will no longer be in a constant state of stress. More minor traumatic events will no longer have a sizeable lasting impact as they will become manageable due to an increase in our emotional well-being.

Physiologically, the brain's response to stress plays a significant role in developing an abused mind. The amygdala, the brain's fear center, is activated when the brain perceives a threat. The amygdala is a small almond-shaped structure in the brain responsible for processing emotions and detecting environmental threats. When we encounter a potential threat, the amygdala sends a signal to the hypothalamus, which activates the body's "fight or flight" response. This response triggers a surge of hormones such as adrenaline and cortisol, which increase heart rate, blood pressure, and respiration to prepare the body for action.

In trauma and abuse, the amygdala can be critical in reinforcing negative thought patterns and beliefs. When a person is exposed to negative stimuli repeatedly through the news, books, movies, social media or other forms of persuasion, the amygdala may become hypersensitive to these stimuli, causing the person to perceive them as even more threatening than they are. This can lead to heightened fear and anxiety, making it more difficult for the person to think critically or objectively (Lebow, H. I. 2021).

The amygdala also plays a role in processing positive stimuli, including rewards and social connections. When we experience something pleasurable or rewarding, such as a delicious meal or a compliment from a friend, the amygdala releases dopamine, a neurotransmitter associated with pleasure and reward. This can help reinforce positive behaviours and beliefs and contribute to developing a more positive mindset.

Stress due to the perception of a threat also affects the brain's prefrontal cortex; rational thought is inhibited, making it difficult for the person to think logically and objectively. The prefrontal cortex is located at the front of the brain and is responsible for executive functions such as decision-making, planning, impulse control, and personality development. When exposed to negative stimuli, the prefrontal cortex can help regulate our emotional responses and prevent us from becoming overwhelmed. Unfortunately, in these negative instances, the prefrontal cortex works against us in unison with the hippocampus by slowing down the process of learning new information to control our fear. We may have difficulty overriding the instinctual flight, fight, and freeze response, and we may also have difficulty thinking logically rather than emotionally.

Furthermore, prolonged exposure to stress and trauma can change the brain's structure and functioning. Chronic stress can cause the hippocampus to shrink, leading to memory and cognitive impairments. The hippocampus is involved in memory formation and can help to encode positive experiences and reinforce positive beliefs. The brain's learning center becomes small and less active when we experience traumas (Lebow, H. I. 2021). This causes issues with memory and problem-solving. Some of us may find it difficult to distinguish between the present and the past, creating a state of hypervigilance. It can also cause the amygdala to become overactive, leading to anxiety, fear, and other negative emotions.

Neurotransmitters, hormones, and other biochemical factors are crucial in shaping the brain's response to negative and positive influences. The release of the hormone cortisol in response to stress can profoundly impact brain function, impairing cognitive performance and reducing the ability to regulate emotions. Similarly, neurotransmitters like dopamine, serotonin, and norepinephrine regulate mood, motivation, and attention. Imbalances in these chemicals can contribute to the development of mental health disorders.

Wounded emotions, a by-product of trauma, can disrupt the balance of neurotransmitters and hormones in the brain, leading to long-term changes in brain function and behaviour. Individuals who have experienced trauma or chronic stress may have lower serotonin levels, which can contribute to symptoms of depression, anxiety, and other mental health problems.

Positive experiences and interventions like therapy, exercise, and meditation can help to restore balance to the brain's biochemical systems, promoting better mental health and resilience. Regular physical activity has been shown to increase neurotransmitters like dopamine and serotonin levels, improving mood and reducing the risk of depression.

Understanding the role of neurotransmitters, hormones, and other biochemical factors in brain function can be a vital step in overcoming wounds in our emotions by cultivating a positive mind. Individuals can take proactive steps towards better mental health and resilience in the face of negative influences by focusing on interventions that support a healthy biochemical balance in the brain (Lebow, H. I. 2021).

One significant factor in the brain's response to positive influences is the release of neurotransmitters and hormones that promote pleasure, happiness, and well-being. These include dopamine, serotonin, oxytocin, and endorphins, among others. When we engage in activities like spending time with loved ones, listening to music, or pursuing our hobbies, the brain releases these feel-good chemicals, reinforcing our positive experiences and promoting a positive outlook.

The other important factor in the brain's response to positive influences is the process of neuroplasticity, which refers to the brain's ability to change and adapt over time in response to new experiences and stimuli. By engaging in activities that promote neuroplasticity, such as learning a new skill, practicing mindfulness, or engaging in creative endeavours, we can actively shape the structure and function of our brains to promote positive thought patterns and behaviours.

We need to recognize the role of social and environmental factors in shaping our mindset and outlook on life. Surrounding ourselves with positive and supportive individuals and engaging in activities that promote community and social connection can profoundly impact our physical and mental health and well-being. Positive interactions can bring healing to an emotional mind. Additionally, exposure to positive role models and inspirational stories can help to shift our perspective and inspire us to cultivate a more positive mindset.

One powerful technique for cultivating a positive mind is the practice of gratitude. By intentionally focusing on the things in our lives that we are grateful for, we can shift our perspective away from negative thoughts and feelings and towards a more optimistic outlook. This can be done through daily journaling, meditation, or simply taking time to reflect on the good things in our lives each day.

As we explore the intricacies of a wounded emotion, addressing the ethical implications of using evidence-based techniques is crucial. We can recondition our minds and restructure what we think to bring proper healing. We must know our triggers and work on diversion methods, grounding techniques, cognitive behavioural therapy, cognitive processing therapy and other evidence-based therapies. We must protect our emotional well-being by protecting our minds from abuse and traumas.

Wounded emotions can have significant and long-lasting effects on an individual's mind and behaviour. While various factors can contribute to an abused mind, it is essential to recognize its impact on our lives, relationships, and work ethics. This can create a vulnerable environment for individuals who have been emotionally wounded.

Developing strategies to discern negative influences can reduce our vulnerability when our emotions are wounded. We must challenge harmful thoughts from ourselves and others that contribute to developing an abusive mind. Promoting values such as critical thinking, empathy, and individualism can create a more inclusive and resilient mind that is less vulnerable to the cause of our emotions being wounded.

Understanding cognitive dissonance is critical in breaking free from emotional wounds. By recognizing the discomfort and tension that arise when beliefs conflict with reality, individuals can begin to challenge and re-evaluate their beliefs. This can be a difficult and uncomfortable process, but it is essential in breaking free from the grip of the cause of being emotionally wounded.

In addition to recognizing cognitive dissonance, various strategies can be employed to overcome it. These include seeking out new information and experiences that challenge existing beliefs, practicing self-reflection and introspection, and seeking the support of trusted friends or professionals. Ultimately, overcoming cognitive dissonance requires a willingness to question deeply held beliefs and face uncomfortable truths, but the reward is an invaluable sense of freedom and autonomy.

NIGHTMARES,
Flashbacks, **AND**
INTRUSIVE THOUGHTS

In the journey towards understanding and healing from trauma, it's essential to explore some perplexing phenomena often experienced by trauma survivors, including nightmares, flashbacks, and intrusive thoughts. These manifestations can be distressing, constantly adding another layer of difficulty to the healing process. This chapter aims to demystify these experiences, providing insights into their origins and offering strategies for coping and management.

Nightmares and flashbacks are common in individuals who have experienced trauma, particularly those with post-traumatic stress disorder (PTSD). Nightmares are distressing dreams related to a traumatic event, often causing the individual to wake up feeling anxious and scared (American Psychiatric Association, 2013). Flashbacks, on the other hand, are vivid and intrusive memories of the traumatic event that can occur during wakefulness, making the individual feel like they are reliving the trauma (Brewin, 2015).

These phenomena can be understood as the brain's attempt to make sense of the traumatic experience. During trauma, the standard processing of experiences can be disrupted, forming fragmented and disorganized memories. These memories can then intrude into consciousness in the form of nightmares and flashbacks, often triggered by reminders of the trauma (Brewin, Gregory, Lipton, & Burgess, 2010).

Intrusive thoughts are another common manifestation of trauma. These are unwanted thoughts, images, or urges related to the traumatic event repeatedly entering the person's mind, causing distress and discomfort. Like nightmares and flashbacks, intrusive thoughts can be seen as a product of disrupted memory processing during trauma.

However, intrusive thoughts are not just memories; they often involve some *interpretation* or *appraisal* of the traumatic event. For instance, the individual might have recurring thoughts about their perceived role in the event, their reactions during the event, or the event's implications for their life and identity. These appraisals can contribute to guilt, shame, fear, and helplessness, perpetuating the distress associated with the trauma.

Managing nightmares, flashbacks, and intrusive thoughts can be challenging but is crucial to healing from trauma. One practical approach is cognitive-behavioural therapy (CBT), which helps individuals change unhelpful thought patterns and develop adaptive coping strategies (Cukor, Olden, Lee, & Difede, 2010).

Nightmare techniques may include imagery rehearsal therapy (IRT), which can be beneficial. This involves changing the ending of the recurring nightmare to a more positive or neutral one and mentally rehearsing the new version (Krakow & Zadra, 2006).

For example, a veteran suffering from recurring nightmares about a battle may use IRT with the guidance of a therapist. Together, they change the ending of the nightmare to one where the veteran helps save a comrade, turning a distressing memory into a positive or empowering one. By repeatedly mentally rehearsing this new version, the veteran begins to experience the altered dream instead of the original nightmare, reducing the emotional distress associated with sleep.

Grounding techniques can be helpful for flashbacks and intrusive thoughts. These techniques aim to bring the individual back to the present moment. They can involve focusing on physical sensations, like touching a piece of fabric, or on the details of the surrounding environment, like naming the colours of the objects in the room (Najavits, 2002).

For example, a car accident survivor experiencing a sudden flashback while driving might use a grounding technique like gripping the steering wheel and focusing on its texture. They may also verbally name the colours and shapes of the cars around them, helping to anchor themselves in the present moment and dissociate from the flashback. They may stop their vehicle and walk on the ground to feel the dirt or gravel under their feet. Some individuals may ground themselves by snapping a rubber band on their wrist, squeezing a stress ball, sitting under the shower, holding ice in their hands and other similar techniques.

Mindfulness-based approaches can help individuals observe intrusive thoughts without judgment or reactivity, reducing their distressing impact (Kearney, McDermott, Malte, Martinez, & Simpson, 2012).

For example, an individual who has experienced trauma from a natural disaster and struggles with constant intrusive thoughts might engage in mindfulness meditation. By observing these thoughts without judgment or reactivity, they can recognize them as transient mental events rather than absolute truths. When an intrusive thought arises, they may practice noting it simply as "a thought" and then return their focus to their breath or another anchor in the present moment. This practice can reduce the distressing impact of the thoughts and promote a sense of control and calm. Sitting back, relaxing, and becoming mindful of oneself is essential in pushing away unwanted thoughts.

Nightmares, flashbacks, and intrusive thoughts can be distressing aspects of the trauma recovery process. However, by understanding their origins and learning effective coping strategies, individuals can start to regain control over these experiences. As we continue exploring trauma and its impacts, it's crucial to remember that these phenomena are not signs of weakness or failure but common responses to extraordinary circumstances. In the next chapter, we will delve into the concept of hypervigilance, another typical response to trauma.

HYPERVIGILANT

In the aftermath of a traumatic event, individuals often find their senses heightened, their alertness increased, and their readiness for danger escalated. This heightened alertness and increased sensitivity to their surroundings is known as hypervigilance. Hypervigilance is a typical response to trauma, yet it is often misunderstood and can add to the distress experienced by trauma survivors. This chapter seeks to demystify hypervigilance, shedding light on its connection to trauma and providing practical strategies for managing it.

Hypervigilance is a state of increased alertness and sensitivity to one's environment. Individuals experiencing hypervigilance may feel constantly 'on edge,' overly aware of their surroundings, and quick to react to potential threats (American Psychological Association, 2013). They may be easily startled, struggle to relax, and find it difficult to focus due to their preoccupation with potential danger.

Hypervigilance is closely linked to the body's fight-or-flight response, a survival mechanism that prepares the body to respond to perceived threats. In the context of trauma, hypervigilance can be understood as a prolonged and heightened activation of this response, even in the absence of actual danger (Charney, 2004).

In the face of trauma, hypervigilance can be seen as the body's attempt to protect itself from further harm. By remaining alert to potential threats, the individual is prepared to respond quickly should danger arise. While this heightened alertness can be adaptive in dangerous situations, problems occur when the threat has passed, but the hypervigilance remains. This can lead to chronic stress, anxiety, and exhaustion, as the individual is constantly in a state of high alert.

Moreover, hypervigilance can significantly impact an individual's quality of life. It can disrupt sleep, impair concentration, and lead to social withdrawal, as the individual may avoid situations or places that trigger their hypervigilance. Over time, this can contribute to developing mental health disorders, such as post-traumatic stress disorder (PTSD) and anxiety disorders (American Psychiatric Association, 2013).

Managing hypervigilance, a heightened state of sensory alertness, is vital to the healing process after trauma. Several evidence-based therapies have benefited those who struggle with hypervigilance.

Cognitive-behavioural Therapy (CBT) helps individuals identify and change unhelpful thought patterns contributing to hypervigilance. Individuals can learn to challenge their overestimation of danger and develop more balanced and realistic appraisals of their environment. For example, someone who has experienced a home burglary might constantly check doors and windows, fearing another break-in. Through CBT, they can learn to recognize that this constant checking is a response to an exaggerated perception of danger, and they can develop strategies to reduce this behaviour, such as setting specific check times and using positive affirmations about their safety (Cukor, Spitalnick, Difede, Rizzo, & Rothbaum, 2009).

Mindfulness and Relaxation Techniques, including deep breathing, progressive muscle relaxation, and mindfulness meditation, can help reduce physiological arousal and promote relaxation, counteracting hypervigilance. A car accident victim might use deep breathing exercises when they feel their heart rate rise as they approach an intersection, the site of their trauma. Focusing on their breath and calming their body can reduce the panic associated with driving through intersections, thus decreasing their overall hypervigilance (Kearney, McDermott, Malte, Martinez, & Simpson, 2012).

Exposure Therapy helps control exposure to triggers in a more controlled setting, which reduces sensitivity to triggers and reduces the intensity of the hypervigilant response. For instance, a military veteran who becomes hypervigilant around loud noises might work with a therapist to gradually expose themselves to controlled loud sounds, slowly desensitizing their reaction and reducing the hypervigilant response (Foa et al., 2006). A police officer may need time to drive by where the shooting occurred. A driver or passenger involved in a motor vehicle accident may require exposure to where the accident occurred to reduce fear and anxiety.

Lifestyle Modifications, which include regular physical exercise, a healthy diet, adequate sleep, and abstaining from stimulants (like caffeine and nicotine), can also help regulate the body's stress response and reduce symptoms of hypervigilance. A nurse working in a high-stress environment might exercise regularly, monitor caffeine intake, and ensure sufficient sleep to maintain a calm and balanced state, thereby minimizing hypervigilance. Even small changes, such as a consistent bedtime routine or incorporating more whole foods into the diet, can make a significant difference in managing hypervigilance (Scott, 2018).

Hypervigilance is a common yet challenging response to trauma. By understanding its origins and learning effective coping strategies, individuals can regain control over their body's stress response, moving towards calm and safety. In the following chapter, we will explore the concept of 'stuck points,' another common hurdle on the path to healing from trauma.

STUCKPOINTS

As we navigate the complex journey of trauma recovery, we often encounter hurdles that seem to halt or slow down our progress. One of these hurdles, known as "stuck points," can be particularly challenging to overcome. Stuck points are places in our thought process where we find ourselves caught in repetitive, negative thinking patterns that impede our healing. This chapter aims to demystify stuck points, highlight their normalcy in the trauma recovery process, and provide practical strategies for overcoming them.

The term "stuck points" originates from cognitive processing therapy (CPT), a specific type of cognitive-behavioral therapy developed to help individuals recover from post-traumatic stress disorder (PTSD) and other trauma-related disorders. In trauma recovery, stuck points are defined as cognitions or beliefs that prevent the individual from recovering (Resick, Monson, & Chard, 2017).

These cognitions often take the form of irrational or maladaptive beliefs about oneself, others, or the world. For example, a trauma survivor might believe they are entirely to blame for their traumatic event or that the world is altogether dangerous. These beliefs can keep the individual stuck in their trauma, hindering their ability to move forward.

Stuck points can occur for various reasons. One of the most significant is the nature of trauma itself. Traumatic events often challenge our fundamental beliefs about the world, such as our sense of safety, justice, or control. When these basic assumptions are shattered, it can lead to cognitive dissonance, a mental conflict where our beliefs no longer align with our experiences.

For example, imagine someone who firmly believes in the inherent goodness of people. If they become a victim of a violent assault, this traumatic event might clash with their pre-existing belief. The dissonance between their belief in human goodness and the cruel reality of their experience creates a mental conflict.

To resolve this dissonance, individuals may adopt new beliefs that align with the traumatic experience but are ultimately maladaptive. These new beliefs might include thoughts like "I can't trust anyone" or "The world is a dangerous place." While these beliefs may make sense in the context of the trauma, they can become stuck points that hinder recovery. They can lead to withdrawal from social connections, increased anxiety, and a restricted life, all of which impede healing.

Stuck points can also arise from attempts to avoid the painful emotions associated with trauma. Facing the whole reality of a traumatic event can be incredibly distressing, and the human mind might seek ways to avoid or minimize this pain.

For example, someone who has lost a child in an accident might cling to believing they could have prevented the tragedy if they had acted differently. This belief might be a way to avoid confronting unbearable grief and guilt. Holding on to this thought, even though it is illogical and self-blaming, might feel less painful than accepting the random and uncontrollable nature of the loss.

By clinging to these maladaptive beliefs, individuals can avoid confronting the whole reality of their trauma and the painful emotions it evokes. However, this avoidance can become a stuck point, preventing them from processing the trauma fully and moving forward.

Overcoming stuck points requires identifying these problematic beliefs and challenging them. This process can be facilitated through therapy, particularly cognitive-behavioural therapies like CPT. These therapies provide structured frameworks to help individuals identify their stuck points, challenge their validity, and develop more adaptive beliefs (Resick et al., 2017).

For instance, a therapist might help the individual identify a stuck point, such as "I am to blame for the trauma." They would then guide the individual to examine the evidence for and against this belief, promoting a more balanced perspective.

In addition to therapy, self-help techniques can also be beneficial. Journaling, for example, can help individuals track their thoughts and identify patterns indicative of stuck points. Mindfulness and meditation practices can promote a non-judgmental awareness of one's thoughts, helping to disengage from maladaptive thinking patterns (Kearncy, McDermott, Malte, Martinez, & Simpson, 2012).

We may want to consider recognizing and understanding the stuck points to break free from stuck points. This might involve identifying specific thoughts or beliefs that are hindering recovery. A therapist who specializes in trauma can help identify and articulate stuck points, providing a safe space to explore these challenges.

Secondly, challenging maladaptive beliefs. Therapies like Cognitive Processing Therapy (CPT) can help challenge and modify the maladaptive beliefs that have become stuck points. Trauma victims must be encouraged to question the accuracy and usefulness of their stuck-point beliefs, which can foster a more flexible and adaptive mindset. If a stuck point is the belief that "I can't trust anyone," a therapist might guide the individual to explore evidence for and against this belief, helping them develop a more nuanced understanding of trust.

Thirdly, emotional processing. Avoidance of painful emotions often underlies stuck points. Gradually confronting and processing these emotions is vital for moving forward. Support from friends, family, or support groups can be instrumental in this process, providing empathy and understanding.

Fourthly, gradually implement exposure therapy. Gradually facing the triggers associated with the trauma (under professional guidance) can help reduce the reaction's intensity and overcome stuck points. This exposure helps build tolerance and reduces sensitivity to triggers, allowing for more adaptive coping.

Fifthly, develop new coping strategies. Learn adaptive coping skills in developing healthy ways to cope with stress and anxiety. This will replace maladaptive beliefs and behaviours. Introducing Mindfulness, Relaxation Techniques, CBT, DBT, Diaphragmic Breathing, Grounding techniques and psychoeducation can help manage anxiety and stay grounded in the present, avoiding overgeneralizing the trauma.

Stuck points are a common and normal part of the trauma recovery process. They reflect the mind's attempts to make sense of traumatic experiences and protect itself from further harm. However, when these attempts become obstacles to healing, it's crucial to identify and address them. With patience, resilience, and the proper support, stuck points can be overcome, paving the way for continued growth and healing.

Trauma can leave lasting marks on an individual, manifesting in a myriad of physical, emotional, cognitive, and behavioural signs and symptoms. Recognizing these signs is the first step towards understanding the impacts of trauma and seeking appropriate help.

There are several physical signs and symptoms that are common among trauma victims. Physical manifestations of trauma can significantly disrupt an individual's daily life and overall health. The most common ones include disruptive sleep patterns. Trauma can significantly disrupt sleep. Insomnia, or difficulty falling or staying asleep, is common among trauma survivors. Nightmares related to the traumatic event can also occur, leading to restless and "unrefreshful" sleep. In some cases, individuals might sleep more than usual to escape or cope (American Psychiatric Association, 2013).

Changes in appetite. Trauma can affect eating habits and appetite. Some individuals might lose their appetite due to stress, anxiety, or feelings of sadness. Others might find comfort in eating and may eat more than usual, potentially leading to weight gain (Yehuda, Neylan, Flory, & McFarlane, 2013).

Somatic complaints. Unexplained physical symptoms, often somatic complaints, are common among individuals who have experienced trauma. These can include headaches, stomach-aches, dizziness, or other physical discomforts that cannot be traced back to a specific physical condition (Gupta, 2013).

Hyperarousal. It's a state of heightened alertness and sensitivity to surroundings that can lead to an exaggerated startle response, restlessness, and feeling constantly 'on edge.' This symptom represents the body's fight-or-flight response, becoming stuck in the 'on' position following a trauma (American Psychological Association, 2013).

Trauma is responsible for emotional signs and symptoms. The emotional impact of trauma can be profound and varied. Some common emotional symptoms include intense fear and anxiety. Trauma survivors may experience extreme fear or anxiety that can be general or related to specific trauma reminders. This fear can manifest as panic attacks, phobias, or a constant sense of dread (American Psychological Association, 2013).

Intrusive thoughts or memories. Individuals may frequently relive the traumatic event in their minds. These intrusive thoughts or memories can be triggered by reminders of the trauma, causing significant distress (Brewin, Gregory, Lipton, & Burgess, 2010).

Mood changes. Trauma can lead to significant changes in mood. These can range from persistent sadness and hopelessness to irritability and anger. Some individuals may also experience emotional numbness or have difficulty experiencing positive emotions (American Psychological Association, 2013).

Feelings of detachment. Some individuals may feel numb or disconnected from others or their own emotions. This detachment can serve as a defence mechanism to protect oneself from painful emotions, but it can also lead to feelings of isolation and loneliness (American Psychological Association, 2013).

Trauma victims experience behavioural signs and symptoms, including avoidance and isolation. Individuals might avoid people, places, or activities that remind them of the trauma. This avoidance can serve as a way to prevent triggering distressing memories or feelings associated with the traumatic event (American Psychological Association, 2013).

There may be changes in personal habits or routines. Individuals may neglect personal hygiene, abandon previously enjoyed hobbies, or change their routines drastically. These changes can reflect the individual's struggle to regain control or cope with distress (American Psychological Association, 2013).

There may be an increase in unhealthy coping strategies, including the misuse of alcohol and prescription medications, illicit drugs, or sexual promiscuity, which can indicate an attempt to numb or distract from the pain of the trauma. While these behaviours may temporarily relieve, they can lead to additional problems, including substance use disorders (National Institute on Drug Abuse, 2020).

Trauma can significantly impact cognitive functioning, which may include difficulty concentrating. The constant state of heightened alertness and intrusive thoughts associated with trauma can make it hard to focus on tasks or keep the mind on one thing. This can affect work or school performance and make daily tasks more challenging (American Psychological Association, 2013).

Memory problems. Some people may have trouble remembering aspects of the trauma. This can result from the mind trying to protect itself from painful memories. In some cases, people might also experience difficulty with memory in general, often due to the high stress and anxiety they are experiencing (Brewin et al., 2010).

Changes in thought patterns: Trauma can lead to persistent negative beliefs about oneself, others, or the world. These can include thoughts like "I am to blame," "The world is entirely dangerous," or "I can't trust anyone." These beliefs can keep individuals stuck in their trauma and hinder their recovery process (Resick, Monson, & Chard, 2017).

Recognizing trauma can be challenging, especially since individuals can react to and cope with trauma in different ways. However, a combination of the above signs—particularly when they persist over time, cause significant distress, or interfere with daily functioning—can indicate trauma.

It's crucial to approach this recognition with empathy and non-judgment, remembering that these signs are normal responses to abnormal events. If you or someone you know exhibits these signs, seeking professional help is essential. Mental health professionals can provide a proper assessment and guide you toward appropriate treatment and support.

Understanding the stuck points, signs and symptoms of trauma is crucial to healing. While these symptoms can be distressing, they testify to our capacity to respond to extraordinary circumstances. As we continue to understand and heal from trauma, we must approach our experiences and those of others with empathy, compassion, and patience. In the following chapter, we will delve into the concept of triggers, exploring how they relate to trauma and how to manage them.

TRIGGERS

In the aftermath of traumatic experiences, individuals often develop certain triggers, specific stimuli that evoke intense emotional responses or bring back distressing memories related to the trauma. These triggers range from certain places, smells, or sounds to particular situations, people, or emotions. Successfully navigating the journey to recovery from trauma requires understanding these triggers and learning practical strategies to manage them.

Understanding triggers in trauma is very important. Triggers are powerful reminders of past traumatic events. They often evoke strong emotional responses and can lead to symptoms of re-experiencing, one of the core features of post-traumatic stress disorder (PTSD) (American Psychiatric Association, 2013). The nature of triggers is highly individualized, depending on the traumatic event and the person's unique experiences and interpretations.

It's essential to remember that the presence of triggers is not a sign of weakness or lack of progress in the healing journey. Instead, they reflect the brain's natural way of associating stimuli with past experiences, especially threatening or harmful ones (van der Kolk, 2015). Recognizing and understanding one's triggers is crucial to managing them effectively. Individuals with traumas are usually triggered by any of their five senses attached to an event responsible for the trauma. It could be smelling, tasting, touching, seeing and hearing.

Triggers are a standard part of the trauma recovery process. While they can be challenging to manage, understanding their nature, identifying personal triggers, and learning effective coping strategies can significantly lessen their impact.

Post-Traumatic Stress Disorder (PTSD) is a complex mental health condition that can manifest in various ways. One critical aspect of PTSD is the role of sensory triggers. These triggers, connected to the five senses—smelling, touching, tasting, seeing, and hearing—can evoke intense memories and reactions related to the trauma (van der Kolk, 2014).

The sense of smell, or olfaction, has a profound connection to memory and emotion, making it a significant factor in understanding PTSD triggers (Herz, 2004). The olfactory system's unique link to the limbic system, which governs emotions, makes smells capable of evoking strong memories and feelings (Herz, 2004). Unlike other senses, the olfactory input bypasses the thalamus and directly reaches the areas of the brain associated with memory and emotion.

Smells can act as powerful cues to recall specific memories, both pleasant and traumatic, which the memory recalls. The emotions tied to these memories can be re-experienced with surprising intensity, even years after the event, which is seen through the emotions. A specific example of this connection can be seen with the smell of burning rubber, which might trigger a flashback for a car accident survivor (Vermetten & Bremner, 2003).

The smell might lead to an immediate and involuntary reliving of the traumatic event, causing anxiety, distress, and physical symptoms like sweating or trembling. This association between smell and trauma can persist, leading to avoidance behaviours, including avoiding places or situations where the smell might be encountered.

Addressing olfactory triggers requires a combination of understanding, coping mechanisms, and therapeutic interventions. The first step is recognizing and becoming aware of the specific smells that act as triggers and understanding their connection to the trauma.

Gradual exposure to the triggering smell in a controlled and supportive environment can help reduce sensitivity (Vermetten & Bremner, 2003). This is when exposure therapy is implemented. Developing coping strategies like deep breathing or mindfulness can help manage the immediate reaction to the trigger. Ongoing support from mental health professionals specializing in trauma can facilitate a more profound healing process.

The sense of smell's role in PTSD is complex and multifaceted. Its direct connection to memory and emotion makes it a powerful and sometimes challenging aspect of trauma recovery. Understanding the underlying neurobiology, recognizing the impact on individuals, and employing evidence-based strategies can help manage olfactory triggers.

By shedding light on this specific sensory connection, we contribute to a broader understanding of PTSD and offer insights that can guide individuals affected by trauma and professionals working in mental health. The olfactory sense is a testament to the intricate ways our brains process and remember experiences, providing a unique window into the human experience of trauma.

Physical sensations and textures can become powerfully connected to traumatic memories (Brewin, 2001). The tactile sense is a potent reminder of specific events and can evoke significant emotional reactions. This section explores the connection between touching and

PTSD, offering insights into understanding, managing, and coping with tactile triggers.

The sense of touch can be linked to objects, environments, or experiences related to the trauma. Textures, temperatures, or physical sensations can all serve as triggers. This is the nature of tactile triggers.

The tactile sensation becomes a conditioned stimulus associated with the traumatic memory. A specific texture might be linked to an object or environment during the traumatic event (Brewin, 2001).

The texture of certain fabrics might remind a veteran of their combat uniform, leading to hypervigilance, panic attacks, or avoidance behaviours. A police officers may be more sensitive to firearms or specific things they were exposed to that can create triggers. It has the same effect on all first responders and those involved in a traumatic event. The triggered response is the emotional response that can include anxiety, distress, and a re-experiencing of the traumatic event.

Managing tactile triggers is very important. This may involve gradually facing the triggering texture in a safe and controlled setting, helping reduce sensitivity over time. Developing new, positive associations with the triggering surface can help break the link with the traumatic memory.

Therapists specializing in trauma can guide individuals in understanding and managing tactile triggers, employing techniques tailored to the individual's specific triggers and reactions. Focusing on present sensations and grounding techniques can help manage the immediate response to a tactile trigger.

Implementing mindfulness techniques and taking a personal approach. Each individual's experience with tactile triggers may be unique. Finding personalized coping strategies, such as carrying an object with a soothing texture, may be beneficial.

The sense of touch, though often overlooked, plays a significant role in the experience of PTSD. Tactile triggers can be complex and deeply intertwined with traumatic memories (Brewin, 2001). Understanding the nature of these triggers, recognizing their impact, and employing strategies to manage and cope with them are essential for healing.

Through professional guidance and individual effort, it's possible to reduce the impact of tactile triggers, fostering a greater sense of control and well-being. This exploration of the sense of touch underscores the multifaceted nature of PTSD and the need for a comprehensive approach to address its unique challenges.

Taste is a sense that often goes beyond mere physical sensation, reaching into cultural, personal, and emotional domains. In the context of PTSD, flavours and foods associated with a traumatic event might become sensory triggers, leading to intense emotional reactions (Herz & Schooler, 2002).

The sense of taste can be intricately tied to specific moments in time, cultural practices, and personal experiences. This connection makes it a potent reminder of specific events or contexts.

Taste often carries cultural significance, and traditional dishes or flavours might be associated with communal or family gatherings. These tastes can become powerful reminders for someone who has experienced trauma in a cultural context.

Taste can also be linked to personal memories and emotions, creating emotional attachments. A specific flavour experienced during a traumatic event may become deeply ingrained, triggering memories and emotional responses.

The way taste can act as a trigger in PTSD is multifaceted. For instance, specific traditional dishes might elicit strong emotional reactions from someone who experienced trauma during a culturally significant event.

Upon encountering the triggering taste, an individual might experience a rush of memories, anxiety, panic, or sadness related to the trauma, considered the immediate reaction.

Over time, the avoidance of specific tastes can lead to dietary restrictions or social withdrawal, especially if the triggering tastes are familiar in the person's cultural or social context.

Addressing taste triggers in PTSD is a delicate process that requires understanding, patience, and tailored strategies.

Under the guidance of a mental health professional, gradual reintroduction of the taste in a controlled and supportive environment can help desensitize the reaction. A gradual reintroduction is essential.

Building positive associations with the triggering flavour can help reduce its connection to trauma. This might involve enjoying the food in a new, safe context or with supportive friends or family.

Cognitive techniques might be employed to challenge and reframe the individual's response to the taste, helping them understand and modify their reaction.

With its deep connections to culture, emotion, and memory, the sense of taste presents unique challenges and opportunities in understanding and managing PTSD triggers. The strategies to address taste triggers must be sensitive to these complexities, offering individualized approaches that acknowledge the profound ways taste can be connected to traumatic experiences (Herz & Schooler, 2002).

Through a combination of professional guidance, gradual exposure, cognitive strategies, and support, individuals can learn to navigate taste triggers, reducing their impact and facilitating healing. Exploring this sensory aspect of PTSD enriches our understanding of trauma's intricate nature and guides the development of compassionate and effective interventions.

Visual cues, such as specific objects, symbols, colours, or environments, can act as potential triggers for PTSD, eliciting flashbacks, anxiety, or other distressing reactions (Hackmann et al., 2004).

The visual cortex's connection to the amygdala, which processes emotions, can cause visual stimuli to evoke strong emotional responses. This is how the brain responds. Visual triggers can be widespread and varied, ranging from specific objects or symbols to broader environments or situations that resemble the traumatic setting. What constitutes a visual trigger can differ significantly among individuals, depending on the nature and context of the trauma.

Seeing a particular type of car involved in an accident might cause intense distress or avoidance behaviours in a survivor. A person who experienced trauma in a crowded place might start to avoid busy areas like shopping malls or public events, significantly impacting daily life.

Most first responders isolate themselves as they fear being placed in a position to assist should something happen when in public. They are more exhausted being out in public and prefer to stay at home.

Pictures, videos, or media resembling the traumatic event can trigger flashbacks or anxiety. People talking about the events leading to the trauma, family and friends asking questions about events, and hearing the news over television or radio are all triggers.

Victims of traumas must learn how to manage visual triggers. Gradual and controlled exposure to the visual trigger, guided by a therapist, can help reduce sensitivity over time (Hackmann et al., 2004).

Techniques that help alter the cognitive response to the visual cue can be used to build resilience and reduce avoidance. This may involve reframing thoughts about the trigger or making new positive associations. Cognitive restructuring is fundamental to stabilize triggers. Mindfulness techniques can be applied to manage the immediate response to a visual trigger, helping the individual stay grounded and present. Adjusting personal or work spaces to minimize exposure to visual triggers can help in the short term while working on long-term coping strategies.

Visual triggers for PTSD encompass various potential stimuli, reflecting the complexity of human vision and perception. The multifaceted nature of visual triggers requires a personalized and comprehensive approach to management.

Understanding each individual's specific nature of visual triggers is vital for developing effective interventions. Through a combination of exposure, cognitive restructuring, mindfulness, and environmental adjustments, individuals with PTSD can learn to navigate these triggers, reducing their impact and facilitating healing.

The exploration of visual triggers adds depth to our understanding of PTSD, illustrating how something as fundamental as sight can become entangled with traumatic memories and reactions. It underscores the need for personalized care and a nuanced approach to treatment, recognizing the unique ways in which each person's visual experience can be affected by trauma.

Auditory stimuli can powerfully evoke memories and reactions related to trauma (Engelhard et al., 2011). This section delves into the nature of auditory triggers, their impact, examples, and strategies for managing them.

Even if not directly linked to the trauma, sounds can become associated through context or repetition. The auditory system's connection to memory centers in the brain allows specific sounds to be strongly tied to emotional experiences.

Auditory triggers can range from distinct noises like gunshots or sirens to more subtle sounds like specific music, voices, or even ambient noise resembling the traumatic event. A particular song playing during a traumatic event might become a trigger, leading to avoidance or emotional distress.

Auditory triggers can affect daily life significantly, causing individuals to avoid places or situations where the sound might occur. This can lead to social isolation, anxiety, or other mental health challenges. It is important to manage auditory triggers and develop healthy means to cope. Gradually and safely exposing trauma victims to the triggering sound in a controlled environment can reduce sensitivity (Engelhard et al., 2011).

Utilizing relaxation techniques when exposed to the trigger can help manage the immediate response. This could include deep breathing, mindfulness, or visualization.

Creating positive associations with positive memories or experiences can help in reconditioning the emotional response from triggers. And working with a mental health professional who understands PTSD and sensory triggers can provide personalized strategies and support.

Hearing is often interconnected with other senses, making the management of auditory triggers complex. For example, a sound might be linked to specific visuals or smells associated with the trauma.

The way auditory triggers affect individuals varies greatly, making a personalized approach essential. What might be a trigger for one person might not affect another, even if the traumatic experiences were similar.

The sense of hearing and its connection to PTSD triggers illustrates trauma's intricate and highly personalized nature. Understanding the role of auditory stimuli in evoking traumatic memories requires a multifaceted approach that recognizes the complexity of human perception and memory. This section provides a comprehensive insight into an essential aspect of trauma recovery by exploring the specific characteristics, examples, and management strategies related to auditory triggers.

The connection between the five senses and PTSD triggers highlights the complexity of trauma and its pervasive impact on daily life. These sensory triggers can affect various aspects of well-being and require a multifaceted approach to management.

Understanding and addressing these triggers is vital for individuals with PTSD and the professionals supporting them. By recognizing the unique role of each sense and developing tailored strategies, it's possible to reduce the impact of these triggers and facilitate healing.

SUPPORT SYSTEM

The path to recovery from trauma can be a long and arduous journey, fraught with numerous challenges and hurdles. Support from loved ones can be crucial in this journey, providing comfort, validation, and strength. This chapter aims to shed light on effective ways to support trauma victims, focusing on the importance of empathy, practical assistance, and the promotion of professional help.

It is essential to have empathy and understanding of trauma and its negative impact on the mind. Supporting a trauma victim starts with compassion and understanding. Empathy involves recognizing and sharing the feelings of another person. In the context of trauma, empathy means acknowledging the trauma victim's experiences, validating their emotions, and showing genuine concern for their wellbeing. It means listening without judgment, offering reassurance, and conveying the message that they are not alone in their struggle.

Understanding entails educating oneself about the nature of trauma and its impacts. It means understanding that trauma can profoundly affect a person's emotions, thoughts, behaviours, and physical health. It also means recognizing that each person's response to trauma is unique and that there is no "right" or "wrong" way to react to or cope with traumatic experiences.

There are practical ways to support those struggling with trauma. Some of these may include listening. Provide a safe space for the trauma victim to share their experiences and emotions. Listen attentively and without judgment. Resist the urge to offer unsolicited advice or try to "fix" their problems. Sometimes, simply being heard can be incredibly healing.

Offer help with everyday tasks. Trauma can disrupt a person's ability to manage daily tasks. Offering help with these tasks, such as cooking, cleaning, or childcare, can alleviate some of their stress and allow them to focus on their healing (APA, 2013).

Encouraging the trauma victim to take care of their physical health. This can involve promoting a balanced diet, regular exercise, adequate sleep, and other self-care practices.

Trauma can make a person feel powerless and out of control. Respecting their boundaries—whether they pertain to physical touch, conversation topics, or personal space—can help them regain a sense of control and safety.

Professional help, including clinical therapy and counselling, can be instrumental in a trauma victim's recovery. Professionals who specialize in trauma can provide evidence-based interventions, such as cognitive-behavioural therapy (CBT), eye movement desensitization and reprocessing (EMDR), and trauma-focused cognitive-behavioural therapy (TF-CBT), that are designed to help individuals process their traumatic experiences and develop effective coping strategies.

Supporting trauma victims in seeking professional help can involve encouraging them to consider therapy, helping them find a suitable professional, offering to accompany them to appointments, and respecting their privacy regarding what they choose to share about their therapy experiences.

Supporting a trauma victim can be delicate, requiring empathy, patience, and understanding. You can make a significant difference in their healing journey by providing emotional support, practical assistance, and encouragement to seek professional help.

First responders such as police officers, firefighters, paramedics, and military personnel are critical in ensuring public safety and health. They are often the first on the scene in emergencies and crises, bearing witness to situations that most of us can hardly imagine. However, this line of duty exposes them to various traumatic experiences, putting them at a heightened risk for trauma-related disorders.

Most first responders would say they accepted trauma as part of the job culture until it became unbearable. The unhealthy coping strategies only work for a period before they become numb to it. The disruptive sleep patterns, changes to their eating habits, inability to concentrate, restlessness, memory issues, hypervigilance, anger, rage, being on the edge, jumpiness and isolation worsen. And the toughness no longer becomes as important as when they started their careers. The Employees Assistant Program, health care benefits available to call a therapist, and other help usually would be considered for weak or broken people, creating a stigma to seek proper support. There are peer support programs within organizations that can be beneficial, fostering a sense of community and mutual understanding (Halpern, Gurevich, Schwartz, & Brazeau, 2009). However, the culture created among first responders has made it challenging to seek help, as no one wants to be labelled as "broken."

Most managers or supervisors in the first responder's sector who do a debriefing after an incident choose their words wisely, commenting, "Everyone is okay, right," blowing off the conversation with a joke to keep things light. However, not everyone deals with traumas the same, especially those who may have children and have experienced a child dying or seen a person killed who may be around the same age as a loved one.

Some of us are kindhearted; trauma can work against us, as we can relate to the victim as our emotions become scared from the experience. We feel the emotional pain and the concepts of grieving, although we are strangers to the victims who may have been killed. There are unique challenges faced by first responders, who, like everyone else, should take time to debrief and process the trauma before pushing themselves back on the road.

First responders encounter unique challenges in their line of work that can contribute to trauma. They are routinely exposed to distressing situations, from natural disasters to violent incidents. This repeated exposure to trauma can lead to the development of Post-Traumatic Stress Disorder (PTSD), anxiety, depression, and other mental health issues (McFarlane & Bryant, 2007).

The nature of the First Responder's work often involves high-stress levels, irregular schedules, and limited opportunities for recovery between traumatic events. These factors can exacerbate the impact of traumatic exposure, leading to chronic stress and burnout (Perrin et al., 2007).

Building resilience is a crucial aspect of supporting first responders. Resilience refers to the ability to adapt and bounce back from adversity and is a critical factor in preventing trauma-related disorders. It can be fostered through various strategies to support trauma victims.

First responders should be encouraged to prioritize self-care. This includes regular physical activity, a healthy diet, adequate sleep, and activities that promote relaxation and stress relief (Benedek, Fullerton, & Ursano, 2007).

Mental health professionals can provide first responders with therapeutic interventions tailored to their unique needs, such as trauma-focused cognitive-behavioural therapy and critical incident stress debriefing (Everly & Lating, 2017).

Organizations can play a crucial role in promoting resilience by providing mental health training, fostering a supportive work environment, and implementing policies that recognize and address the psychological risks associated with first responder work (Paton & Violanti, 2007).

First responders serve an invaluable role in our society, often at a tremendous personal cost. Our collective responsibility is to ensure they have the necessary support and resources to cope with the unique challenges of their work. By understanding these challenges and implementing strategies to build resilience, we can help first responders maintain their mental health and continue their vital service to the community.

The impact of trauma is far-reaching, often extending beyond the individual who directly experienced the traumatic event. Spouses or partners of trauma victims may find themselves in a challenging position, trying to provide support while dealing with their emotional responses.

Secondary trauma, also known as vicarious trauma or compassion fatigue, is the emotional distress that results from exposure to another person's traumatic experiences. It is common among those who are in close relationships with trauma victims, including spouses or partners. They might find themselves deeply affected by hearing about their loved one's traumatic experiences or observing their distress.

Symptoms of secondary trauma can mirror those of primary trauma, including emotional exhaustion, intrusive thoughts, difficulty sleeping, and changes in mood or outlook. It's essential for spouses or partners to recognize these symptoms and understand that they are familiar and valid responses to their situation.

Self-care can often take a backseat while supporting a loved one through trauma. However, it's crucial for spouses or partners to maintain their well-being to provide adequate support.

Maintaining healthy boundaries is essential to avoid burnout. Understanding the difference between supporting and taking on your loved one's trauma is crucial. While being empathetic and present is necessary, try not to carry their emotional burden as your own. This may require setting emotional and even physical boundaries.

Engaging in activities that can reduce stress should be an important entity to consider. Regular exercise, a healthy diet, adequate sleep, and relaxation techniques such as mindfulness, yoga, or meditation can help manage stress levels (Tanielian et al., 2013).

Staying connected with others and avoiding isolation will help in recovery. Maintaining social connections outside the relationship can provide additional emotional support and a sense of normalcy. This could involve spending time with friends, participating in social activities, or joining a support group for spouses or partners of trauma victims (Cerel, Padgett, Conwell, & Reed, 2009).

Seeking professional help can be vital for spouses or partners of trauma victims, especially if they are experiencing symptoms of secondary trauma. Therapists can provide a safe space to express feelings, offer strategies to cope with stress, and provide guidance on supporting their loved ones. Couple therapy can also be beneficial, providing a structured environment for communication and mutual understanding (Sautter et al., 2009).

Moreover, mental health professionals can provide or recommend resources, such as support groups or educational materials, to help spouses or partners better understand trauma and its impacts. These resources can be invaluable in equipping them to provide practical support to their loved ones while caring for their mental health.

Supporting a loved one through trauma is a journey that requires patience, compassion, and self-care. Spouses or partners need to remember that their feelings are valid and that taking care of their mental health is not a sign of selfishness but a necessity. Understanding secondary trauma, implementing self-care strategies, and seeking professional help can navigate this journey with resilience and strength.

Supporting a loved one through trauma can be challenging, filled with uncertainty and emotional complexity. As a spouse or partner, you may find yourself unsure of how to respond or what to do to help. We need to know how to respond to our loved one's trauma, with a focus on empathy, active listening, and providing support at a pace that respects your loved one's needs and boundaries.

Trauma can elicit a wide range of responses, all-natural reactions to unnatural events. Your loved one may experience emotional upheaval, changes in behaviour, or even physical symptoms. They may withdraw, seem unusually irritable, or have difficulty sleeping. They may also re-experience their trauma through flashbacks or nightmares (American Psychological Association, 2013).

It's crucial to understand that these responses are part of their healing process and are not reflective of any personal failings. They are coping with a profoundly distressing and disruptive event, and their reactions are their body and mind's way of processing this experience.

Empathy and active listening are two of the most powerful tools to support your loved one. Empathy involves trying to understand and share their feelings. This doesn't mean you must have experienced trauma yourself, but rather that you make an effort to imagine what they might be feeling and respond with compassion (Decety & Jackson, 2004).

Active listening involves entirely focusing on your loved one when they speak, showing that you're engaged and interested. This can involve nonverbal cues such as nodding, maintaining eye contact, and verbal affirmations such as "I see" or "I understand." It's also vital to avoid interrupting or offering unsolicited advice.

We need to provide support without pushing. While you naturally want to help your loved one, it's essential to avoid pushing them to share more than they're comfortable with or to move faster in their recovery than they're ready for. Everyone's healing process is different, and what works for one person might not work for another.

Be patient and let them set the pace. Offer support and be there for them, but respect their boundaries and need for space. Encourage them to seek professional help, but understand that the decision is ultimately theirs (Briere & Scott, 2014).

Supporting a loved one through trauma can be challenging, but with patience, empathy, and understanding, you can provide meaningful support. Remember that it's also essential to take care of your own mental health, and don't hesitate to seek support for yourself if you need it. In the following chapter, we will delve deeper into the concept of 'recovery,' exploring what it means in the context of trauma and how it can be fostered.

The process of healing from trauma is often complex and multifaceted, involving personal resilience and external support. While friends, family, and self-care strategies play a crucial role, professional support provides a cornerstone in the recovery journey. The importance of professional support for individuals grappling with trauma, its benefits, the different types of assistance available, and indications for seeking help are necessary.

Professional support, such as therapists, psychologists, psychiatrists, and other mental health professionals, can offer targeted, evidence-based interventions tailored to individuals' unique needs and experiences. They provide a safe, confidential environment for individuals to express and process their feelings, thoughts, and fears related to their traumatic experiences.

These professionals are trained to understand the nuanced effects of trauma on the mind and body. They can guide individuals through the process of understanding and making sense of their experiences. They can help individuals build resilience, develop coping mechanisms, and work towards post-traumatic growth, a positive psychological change experienced due to the struggle with highly challenging life circumstances (Tedeschi & Calhoun, 2004).

Seeking professional help offers a range of benefits for individuals healing from trauma. As mentioned, a professional can assist with symptom management by introducing several evidence-based therapies. Therapies such as Cognitive Behavioral Therapy (CBT) and Eye Movement Desensitization and Reprocessing (EMDR) have been proven effective in reducing symptoms of Post-Traumatic Stress Disorder (PTSD), such as flashbacks, nightmares, and intrusive thoughts (Cukor et al., 2009).

Professionals can create a safe place where traumas can be processed. Professional help provides a secure, non-judgmental space for individuals to process their traumatic experiences, which can be instrumental in the healing process (Briere & Scott, 2014).

Mental health professionals can provide individuals with effective coping strategies to manage triggers and stress, enhancing their ability to function in daily life (Resick et al., 2008).

Early intervention with professional support can lead to better long-term recovery outcomes, reducing the risk of chronic PTSD or associated conditions such as depression and anxiety (Rothbaum et al., 2000).

There are a variety of professional support options that cater to individuals' distinct needs. In individual therapy, a person meets one-on-one with a trained therapist in a safe, caring, and confidential environment. This setting allows personalized attention and treatment tailored to the individual's unique needs and situation (Cukor et al., 2009).

Individual therapy can provide deep, personalized healing and is adaptable to the person's specific needs and pace. The individualized attention allows for a solid therapeutic relationship.

Individual therapy can be more costly than group options. Some people may feel isolated or like they are the "only one" with their experience.

In group therapy, one or more therapists lead a group of individuals facing similar issues. Group members can share experiences, learn from each other, and practice new skills in a safe and supportive environment. For instance, a group therapy session for trauma survivors might focus on sharing coping strategies or providing mutual support and understanding (Yalom & Leszcz, 2005).

Group therapy allows individuals to learn from each other's experiences and provides a sense of community. It can also be more affordable than individual therapy. Some people may feel uncomfortable sharing personal experiences in a group setting. The group's needs might not align perfectly with an individual's needs.

Psychiatrists can provide medical evaluations, diagnose mental health conditions, and manage medication. A psychiatrist might prescribe antidepressants or anti-anxiety medications to help manage severe symptoms related to trauma, including extreme anxiety or depression (Bernardy & Friedman, 2015).

Psychiatrists can provide medication, a beneficial adjunct to therapy for managing severe or persistent symptoms. They can also diagnose and treat co-occurring mental health conditions. Medication can have side effects and does not resolve the underlying issues or teach coping skills. Also, psychiatry services can be expensive and not always covered by insurance.

Support groups provide a space for people to share personal experiences and feelings, coping strategies, or firsthand information about diseases or treatments. They can often complement professional therapies. For instance, a trauma survivor might attend a support group to connect with others who have gone through similar experiences and to share their coping strategies (Salzer et al., 2010).

Support groups provide a sense of community and understanding. They can be empowering, and they are often free or low-cost. Support groups are typically not led by professionals, so they do not provide professional therapy or medical advice. The support quality can vary depending on the group's composition and leadership.

Knowing when to seek professional help is crucial. Generally, it's advisable to consider professional support when trauma symptoms persist for over a month and interfere with daily functioning. When your experiences lead to intense distress or physical symptoms, especially when reminded of the trauma. There are feelings of being stuck in the recovery process or having difficulty navigating it alone. And you are experiencing suicidal thoughts or self-harming ideations.

Professional support plays a pivotal role in the journey of healing from trauma. The benefits it provides—symptom management and effective coping strategies to a safe space for processing trauma—can significantly contribute to recovery. While the decision to seek professional help is profoundly personal and depends on individual circumstances, knowing the options available and when to consider them can be beneficial.

RETURN *to* WORK

Work is a significant aspect of many people's lives, providing financial security, a sense of purpose, routine, and social interaction. However, for individuals recovering from trauma, the question of when to return to work can be fraught with uncertainty and anxiety. There needs to be thoughtful considerations involved in this decision with guidance on facilitating a triumphant return to work after trauma.

Work can play a complex role in trauma recovery. On the one hand, returning to work can provide a sense of normalcy and routine, which can be grounding for individuals who have experienced trauma. It can also offer a sense of purpose and accomplishment and provide an opportunity for social interaction, which can benefit mental health (Savickas, 2011).

On the other hand, returning to work too soon or in an unsupportive environment can exacerbate stress and potentially hinder recovery. The workplace may also hold reminders of the traumatic event, mainly if the trauma occurred at work or is related to the individual's job role (Bhui et al., 2005).

Assessing readiness to return to work after trauma is a complex process that should be considered. Psychological readiness ensures that the trauma victim has made sufficient progress in their recovery to manage the stress and demands of work. And they can regulate their emotions and cope with potential triggers in the workplace. (Corrigan & Watson, 2003).

Physical readiness is essential to ensure the trauma victim's physical health has been improved. And that the physical injury has recovered to a level that allows them to carry out their duties safely and effectively.

The trauma victims must have adequate support systems in place, both in the workplace and outside, to assist them in their return to work.

The assessment of readiness should ideally involve input from the individual, their therapist or mental health professional, and, if appropriate, their employer or occupational health representative.

A gradual return to work can help mitigate the stress of transitioning back into the work environment. This might involve starting with part-time hours or lighter duties and gradually increasing work demands as the individual's capacity improves (Waddell & Burton, 2006).

Developing a return-to-work plan in collaboration with the employer and any involved healthcare professionals can also be helpful. This plan might include strategies for managing potential triggers in the workplace, modifications to work duties or environment, and arrangements for ongoing support (e.g., regular check-ins with a supervisor or access to counselling services).

Employers can play a crucial role in facilitating a triumphant return to work after trauma, making reasonable accommodations, such as adjusting work hours or duties, to support the individual's recovery (Job Accommodation Network, 2020).

Fostering a supportive work environment where the individual feels safe and understood. This might involve educating managers and colleagues about trauma or setting up a peer support network within the workplace (American Institute of Stress, 2017).

Providing access to resources and support, such as Employee Assistance Programs (EAPs) or occupational health services, can assist individuals in managing their mental health at work (Employee Assistance Professionals Association, 2014).

Returning to work after trauma is a significant milestone in the recovery journey. It requires careful consideration of the individual's psychological and physical readiness, a gradual approach, and an understanding and supportive work environment. Returning to work can be a positive step towards recovery and normalcy with these elements in place.

CONCLUSION

In conclusion, it is essential to reflect on the journey we've undertaken. From understanding the nuanced nature of trauma to delving into the experiences of trauma victims to exploring the complex path of recovery—each step has shed light on the profound and far-reaching impacts of trauma.

The individuality of trauma experiences is important to consider. Each trauma victim will have a different recovery time. Trauma is a deeply personal and subjective experience. What constitutes a traumatic event for one person might not be the same for another. Similarly, individuals' responses to trauma can vary widely, influenced by various factors such as their personality, past experiences, and social support networks.

Empathy and understanding are crucial whether you're a trauma victim, a friend, a family member, or a professional providing support. These qualities enable us to validate the trauma victim's experiences, provide effective support, and foster an environment conducive to healing.

Professional help can play a critical role in trauma recovery. Therapists and counsellors trained in trauma can provide evidence-based interventions tailored to the individual's needs, helping them process their traumatic experiences and develop effective coping strategies.

Self-care is not a luxury but a necessity in the trauma recovery journey. Taking care of one's physical and mental health, nurturing resilience, and cultivating healthy coping mechanisms are essential aspects of healing from trauma.

Healing from trauma is not a linear journey. It's a path marked by ups and downs, progress, and setbacks. It's important to remember that experiencing setbacks does not signify failure but is a normal part of the healing process. Everyone moves at their own pace, and each small step forward is a testament to their strength and resilience.

Support systems—comprising family, friends, therapists, and community resources—can be a lifeline for individuals navigating the trauma recovery journey. The presence of supportive and understanding individuals who validate their experiences can make a significant difference in a trauma victim's healing process.

Understanding trauma and its impacts is an ongoing journey. Trauma research is continually evolving, with new insights and therapeutic approaches emerging. It's essential for all of us, whether we're trauma victims, loved ones, or professionals, to continue learning and expanding our understanding.

As we conclude this guide, let us part with a message of hope and resilience. The journey to recovery from trauma may be fraught with challenges, but it is also a journey of healing, growth, and rediscovery. It's a journey that underscores the strength of the human spirit and its capacity to heal.

Remember, you are not alone. Resources, people who want to help, and a whole community rooting for your recovery are available. No matter how small, each step you take is a step toward healing; it's a step from "Trauma To Triumph." And with the proper support, time, and care, recovery is within your reach.

References

American Institute of Stress. (2017). Critical incident stress management programs for the workplace.

American Psychiatric Association. (2013). Diagnostic and statistical manual of mental disorders (5th ed.).

American Psychological Association. (2013). Recognition of Psychotherapy Effectiveness. Psychotherapy, 50(1), 102–109.

American Psychological Association. (2013). Trauma. In APA Dictionary of Psychology. http://dictionary.apa.org/trauma

APA Presidential Task Force on Evidence-Based Practice. (2006). Evidence-based practice in psychology. American Psychologist, 61(4), 271–285.

Bernardy, N. C., & Friedman, M. J. (2015). Psychopharmacological strategies in the management of posttraumatic stress disorder

(PTSD): what have we learned?. Current psychiatry reports, 17(4), 20.

Bhui, K. S., Dinos, S., Stansfeld, S. A., & White, P. D. (2005). A synthesis of the evidence for managing stress at work: a review of the reviews reporting on anxiety, depression, and absenteeism. Journal of environmental and public health, 2012.

Bisson, J. I., Roberts, N. P., Andrew, M., Cooper, R., & Lewis, C. (2013). Psychological therapies for chronic post-traumatic stress disorder (PTSD) in adults. Cochrane Database of Systematic Reviews, (12).

Bloom, S. L. (2013). Creating Sanctuary: Toward the Evolution of Sane Societies (Revised edition). Routledge.

Brewin, C. R., Gregory, J. D., Lipton, M., & Burgess, N. (2010). Intrusive images in psychological disorders: Characteristics, neural mechanisms, and treatment implications. Psychological Review, 117(1), 210-232.

Brewin, C. R. (2015). Re-experiencing traumatic events in PTSD: New avenues in research on intrusive memories and flashbacks. European Journal of Psychotraumatology, 6(1), 27180.

Brewin, C. R. (2001). A cognitive neuroscience account of posttraumatic stress disorder and its treatment. *Behaviour Research and Therapy*, 39(4), 373-393.

Briere, J., & Scott, C. (2014). Principles of trauma therapy: A guide to symptoms, evaluation, and treatment (2nd ed.). SAGE Publications.

Centre for Addiction and Mental Health. (2019). Types of Trauma and Violence. https://www.camh.ca/en/health-info/mental-illness-and-addiction-index/trauma

Charney, D. S. (2004). Psychobiological mechanisms of resilience and vulnerability: Implications for successful adaptation to extreme stress. American Journal of Psychiatry, 161(2), 195-216.

Cloitre, M., Courtois, C. A., Ford, J. D., Green, B. L., Alexander, P., Briere, J., Herman, J. L., Lanius, R., Stolbach, B. C., Spinazzola, J., Van der Kolk, B. A., & Van der Hart, O. (2012). The ISTSS Expert Consensus Treatment Guidelines for Complex PTSD in Adults.

Cloitre, M., Miranda, R., Stovall-McClough, K. C., & Han, H. (2005). Beyond PTSD: Emotion regulation and interpersonal problems as predictors of functional impairment in survivors of childhood abuse. Behavior Therapy, 36(2), 119-124.

Cohen, J. A., Mannarino, A. P., & Deblinger, E. (2006). Treating Trauma and Traumatic Grief in Children and Adolescents. Guilford Press.

Cook, A., Blaustein, M., Spinazzola, J., & van der Kolk, B. (Eds.). (2005). Complex Trauma in Children and Adolescents. National Child Traumatic Stress Network. http://www.NCTSNet.org.

Corrigan, J. D., & Watson, J. D. (2003). Factors that influence return to work after traumatic brain injury. NeuroRehabilitation, 18(3), 199-208.

Courtois, C. A. (2004). Complex trauma, complex reactions: Assessment and treatment. Psychotherapy: Theory, Research, Practice, Training, 41(4), 412–425.

Cukor, J., Spitalnick, J., Difede, J., Rizzo, A., & Rothbaum, B. O. (2009). Emerging treatments for PTSD. Clinical Psychology Review, 29(8), 715-726.

REFERENCES

Cukor, J., Olden, M., Lee, F., & Difede, J. (2010). Evidence-based treatments for PTSD, new directions, and special challenges. Annals of the New York Academy of Sciences, 1208(1), 82-89.

Danese, A., & McEwen, B. S. (2012). Adverse childhood experiences, allostasis, allostatic load, and age-related disease. Physiology & Behavior, 106(1), 29-39.

Decety, J., & Jackson, P. L. (2004). The functional architecture of human empathy. Behavioral and cognitive neuroscience reviews, 3(2), 71-100.

Elliot, D. E., Bjelajac, P., Fallot, R. D., Markoff, L. S., & Reed, B. G. (2005). Trauma-informed or trauma-denied: Principles and implementation of trauma-informed services for women. Journal of Community Psychology, 33(4), 461–477.

Employee Assistance Professionals Association. (2014). The role of employee assistance programs (EAPs) in assisting organizations in times of workplace trauma.

Engelhard, I. M., van den Hout, M. A., & Smeets, M. A. M. (2011). Taxing working memory reduces vividness and emotional intensity of images about the Queen's Day tragedy. *Journal of Behavior Therapy and Experimental Psychiatry*, 42(1), 32-37.

Everly, G. S., & Lating, J. M. (2017). The Johns Hopkins Guide to Psychological First Aid. JHU Press.

Foa, E. B., Huppert, J. D., & Cahill, S. P. (2006). Emotional Processing Theory: An Update. In B. O. Rothbaum (Ed.), Pathological Anxiety: Emotional Processing in Etiology and Treatment (pp. 3-24). Guilford Press.

Foa, E. B., Hembree, E. A., & Rothbaum, B. O. (2007). Prolonged Exposure Therapy for PTSD: Emotional Processing of

Traumatic Experiences, Therapist Guide. Oxford University Press.

Ford, J. D., & Courtois, C. A. (2009). Defining and understanding complex trauma and complex traumatic stress disorders. In C. A. Courtois & J. D. Ford (Eds.), Treating complex traumatic stress disorders: An evidence-based guide (p. 13–30). The Guilford Press.

Hackmann, A., Ehlers, A., Speckens, A., & Clark, D. M. (2004). Characteristics and content of intrusive memories in PTSD and their changes with treatment. *Journal of Traumatic Stress*, 17(3), 231-240.

Hall, S. A., Brodar, K. E., LaBar, K. S., Berntsen, D., & Rubin, D. C. (2018). Neural responses to emotional involuntary memories in posttraumatic stress disorder: Differences in timing and activity. NeuroImage. Clinical, 19, 793–804.

Halpern, J., Gurevich, M., Schwartz, B., & Brazeau, P. (2009). What makes an incident critical for ambulance workers? Emotional outcomes and implications for intervention. Work & Stress, 23(2), 173-189.

Herz, R. S. (2004). A naturalistic analysis of autobiographical memories triggered by olfactory visual and auditory stimuli. *Chemical Senses*, 29(3), 217-224.

Herz, R. S., & Schooler, J. W. (2002). A naturalistic study of autobiographical memories evoked by olfactory and visual cues: Testing the Proustian hypothesis. *The American Journal of Psychology*, 115(1), 21-32.

Hofmann, S. G., Asnaani, A., Vonk, I. J., Sawyer, A. T., & Fang, A. (2012). The Efficacy of Cognitive Behavioral Therapy: A Review of Meta-analyses. Cognitive Therapy and Research, 36(5), 427–440.

REFERENCES

Hodas, G. R. (2006). Responding to Childhood Trauma: The Promise and Practice of Trauma Informed Care. Pennsylvania Office of Mental Health and Substance Abuse Services.

Job Accommodation Network. (2020). Accommodation and Compliance: Post-Traumatic Stress Disorder (PTSD).

Jowett, S., Karatzias, T., Shevlin, M., & Albert, I. (2020). Differentiating symptom profiles of ICD-11 PTSD, complex PTSD, and borderline personality disorder: A latent class analysis in a multiply traumatized sample. Personality disorders, 11(1), 36–45.

Kearney, D. J., McDermott, K., Malte, C., Martinez, M., & Simpson, T. L. (2012). Association of participation in a mindfulness program with measures of PTSD, depression and quality of life in a veteran sample. Journal of Clinical Psychology, 68(1), 101-116.

Krakow, B., & Zadra, A. (2006). Clinical management of chronic nightmares: Imagery rehearsal therapy. Behavioral Sleep Medicine, 4(1), 45-70.

Lebow, H. I. (2021, July 2). *How does PTSD affect the brain? the physical effects of trauma.* Psych Central. Retrieved March 27, 2023, from https://psychcentral.com/ptsd/the-science-behind-ptsd-symptoms-how-trauma-changes-the-brain?slot_pos=article_1&utm_source=Sailthru+Email&utm_medium=Email&utm_campaign=weekly&utm_content=2023-01-25&apid=&rvid=a61d340305c0c28b12afbde3d63c30d3d9ae4dc9399ad609dd609e81b5119a9e combat-related PTSD.

sciencedirect.com/science/article/pii/S2213158218301190

Maercker, A., Cloitre, M., Bachem, R., Schlumpf, Y.R., Khoury, B., Hitchcock, C., & Bohus, M. (2022). Complex post-traumatic stress disorder. The Lancet, 400, 60-72.

McFarlane, A. C., & Bryant, R. A. (2007). Post-traumatic stress disorder in occupational settings: anticipating and managing the risk. Occupational Medicine, 57(6), 404-410.

Meiser-Stedman, R., McKinnon, A., Dixon, C., Boyle, A., Smith, P., & Dalgleish, T. (2017). Acute stress disorder and the transition to posttraumatic stress disorder in children and adolescents: Prevalence, course, prognosis, diagnostic suitability, and risk markers. Depression and anxiety, 34(4), 348–355.

National Institute of Mental Health. (2019). Post-Traumatic Stress Disorder. https://www.nimh.nih.gov/health/topics/post-traumatic-stress-disorder-ptsd/index.shtml

Najavits, L. M. (2002). Seeking safety: A treatment manual for PTSD and substance abuse. Guilford Press.

National Institute of Mental Health. (2020). Post-Traumatic Stress Disorder. NIMH.

Nolen-Hoeksema, S., & Watkins, E. R. (2011). A heuristic for developing transdiagnostic models of psychopathology: Explaining multifinality and divergent trajectories. Perspectives on Psychological Science, 6(6), 589-609.

Paton, D., & Violanti, J. M. (2007). Working in high risk environments: Developing sustained resilience. Charles C Thomas Publisher.

Patel, R., Spreng, R. N., Shin, L. M., & Girard, T. A. (2012). Neurocircuitry models of posttraumatic stress disorder and beyond: A meta-analysis of functional neuroimaging studies. Neuroscience & Biobehavioral Reviews, 36(9), 2130-2142.

Pennebaker, J. W., & Smyth, J. M. (2016). Opening up by writing it down: How expressive writing improves health and eases emotional pain. Guilford Publications.

Perrin, M. A., DiGrande, L., Wheeler, K., Thorpe, L., Farfel, M., & Brackbill, R. (2007). Differences in PTSD prevalence and associated risk factors among World Trade Center disaster rescue and recovery workers. American journal of psychiatry, 164(9), 1385-1394.

Raise-Abdullahi, P., Meamar, M., Vafaei, A. A., Alizadeh, M., Dadkhah, M., Shafia, S., Ghalandari-Shamami, M., Naderian, R., Afshin Samaei, S., & Rashidy-Pour, A. (2023). Hypothalamus and Post-Traumatic Stress Disorder: A Review. Brain sciences, 13(7), 1010.

Resick, P. A., Monson, C. M., & Chard, K. M. (2017). Cognitive Processing Therapy for PTSD: A Comprehensive Manual. Guilford Press.

Rothbaum, B. O., Meadows, E. A., Resick, P., & Foy, D. W. (2000). Cognitive-Behavioral Therapy. In E. B. Foa, T. M. Keane, & M. J. Friedman (Eds.), Effective treatments for PTSD: Practice guidelines from the International Society for Traumatic Stress Studies (p. 60–83)

Salzer, M. S., Schwenk, E., & Brusilovskiy, E. (2010). Certified peer specialist roles and activities: results from a national survey. Psychiatric services, 61(5), 520-523.

Sareen, J. (2007). Physical and mental comorbidity, disability, and suicidal behavior associated with posttraumatic stress disorder in a large community sample. Psychosomatic Medicine, 69(3), 242-248.

Sautter, F. J., Glynn, S. M., Thompson, K. E., Franklin, L., & Han, X. (2009). A couple-based approach to the reduction of PTSD avoidance symptoms: Preliminary findings. Journal of marital and family therapy, 35(3), 343-349.

Savickas, M. L. (2011). Career counseling. American Psychological Association.

Scott, E. (2018). The Impact of Stress on Your Body. Verywell Mind.

Shapiro, F. (2001). Eye Movement Desensitization and Reprocessing: Basic Principles, Protocols, and Procedures (2nd ed.). Guilford Press.

Sledjeski, E. M., Speisman, B., & Dierker, L. C. (2008). Does number of lifetime traumas explain the relationship between PTSD and chronic medical conditions? Answers from the National Comorbidity Survey-Replication (NCS-R). Journal of Behavioral Medicine, 31(4), 341-349.

Stubley, J., & Young, L. (Eds.). (2021). Complex Trauma: The Tavistock Model (1st ed.). Routledge.

Substance Abuse and Mental Health Services Administration (SAMHSA). (2014). SAMHSA's Concept of Trauma and Guidance for a Trauma-Informed Approach.

Tanielian, T., Jaycox, L. H., Adamson, D. M., Burnam, M. A., Burns, R. M., Caldarone, L. B., ... & Vaiana, M. E. (2013). Invisible wounds of war: Psychological and cognitive injuries, their consequences, and services to assist recovery. Rand Corporation.

Teicher, M. H., Samson, J. A., Anderson, C. M., & Ohashi, K. (2016). The effects of childhood maltreatment on brain structure, function and connectivity. Nature Reviews Neuroscience, 17(10), 652-666.

van der Kolk, B. A. (2014). The body keeps the score: Brain, mind, and body in the healing of trauma. Viking.

REFERENCES

Vermetten, E., & Bremner, J. D. (2003). Olfaction as a traumatic reminder in posttraumatic stress disorder: Case reports and review. *The Journal of Clinical Psychiatry*, 64(2), 202-207.

Waddell, G., & Burton, A. K. (2006). Is work good for your health and well-being?. The Stationery Office.

Yalom, I. D., & Leszcz, M. (2005). The theory and practice of group psychotherapy. Basic Books.